SO-EKN-741

SEWING FOR BABY

by Kerstin Martensson

ISBN 0-913212-10-5

About the Author

SEWING FOR BABY is the twelfth book in a series of books on home sewing by Kerstin Martensson. Her previous best selling books have achieved world-wide success and popularity. The overwhelming acceptance of Kerstin Martensson's books can be attributed to their illustrated, easy-to-follow, step-by-step procedures. Over a million copies of her books have been sold thus far. Many of these are being used by schools and colleges throughout the western world as sewing textbooks.

Kerstin Martensson is the President of KWIK·SEW Pattern Co., Inc., and is internationally known as one of the foremost home economists. Kerstin was born in Gothenburg, Sweden and educated in both Sweden and England. She specialized in clothing construction, pattern design and fashion.

Kerstin has traveled extensively throughout the United States, Canada, Australia, England and the Scandinavian countries lecturing on her techniques to make sewing faster, easier and more fun.

Kerstin founded KWIK•SEW Pattern Co., Inc., in 1968 to make patterns for stretch fabric as at that time none of the established pattern companies had patterns for this type of fabric. The company has grown into a world-wide operation with subsidiaries or offices in Australia, Canada and Europe. There are over eight hundred patterns in the KWIK•SEW pattern line and the line now includes patterns for all types of fabric.

KWIK•SEW Pattern company's growth has been credited to the patterns easy construction methods which enable the sewer to make professional looking garments in the least amount of time. The customers have come to depend on KWIK•SEW for great fit and styling. All the patterns are multi-sized and have four or five sizes in each pattern. KWIK•SEW has the largest and best selection of patterns for babies, toddlers, boys and girls. The newest addition to the KWIK•SEW pattern line are Kwik Serge patterns which are especially designed for the serger (overlock) machine and they can be made completely on the serger. All these patterns have dual instructions for both the standard and the serger (overlock) machines.

Kerstin is encouraged by her customers' overwhelming response to her patterns and books, and she is dedicated to bringing the most up-to-date fashion and sewing techniques to the home sewer.

Introduction

A NEW BABY - how wonderful! You will have so much fun sewing for that special baby. All it takes is a good pattern, a little fabric, a little time and love. It is fun to show off a baby with adorable outfits made by you. You can dress your baby any way you choose. It will not always be this way because in just a few years, they will have their own ideas as to what they wish to wear.

You can use a great variety of fabrics, appliques, laces and other trims. It used to be that all little girls were dressed in pink and the boys in blue. This is no longer so. All types of fabrics and colors are now used for both boy and girl babies. Just remember to choose soft materials as babies have very soft, sensitive skin.

Our goal for writing this book is to provide you with all the patterns you need for the baby's first year with up-to-date and complete instructions for sewing these garments. We have included fabric information, yardage requirements, cutting instructions and the correct stitches to use for the different fabrics. The book includes step-by-step instructions for all the garments and with beautifully illustrated artwork.

The book has eight sections. The first section has general sewing information. Section Two contains cutting and sewing instructions for baby's nursery items. You will be able to create a beautiful nursery to welcome the baby home. The last section has thirty-five appliques which can be used on all the garments and nursery items. The remaining sections have complete cutting and sewing instructions for at least thirty garments plus many variations.

The easy-to-follow instructions and clear illustrations will enable even the beginner sewer to make professional garments. The advanced sewer will be able to create additional variations since most of the pattern pieces are interchangeable.

See for yourself how fast, easy and fun SEWING FOR BABY can be.

The tiny baby,
sweet and new,
can make the biggest
dreams come true.

Contents

SECTION 1 GENERAL SEWING INFORMATION . . 9
Stretch Charts 11
Pattern Information 11
Cutting 13
Thread 15
Sewing 15
Seams 16
Bias Tape 18
Hemming 18
Pressing 19
Snaps, Buttons and Buttonholes . . . 20

SECTION 2 AT THE VERY BEGINNING 21
Crib Sheet 22
Receiving Blanket 23
Bath Towel with Hood 24
Bibs 25
Bumper Pads 29
Comforter 31

SECTION 3 SLEEPERS, KIMONOS 33
Sleeper 34
Kimono 39

SECTION 4 T-SHIRTS, ROMPERS, PANTIES 41
T-shirt with set-in sleeves 42
Ribbing Neckband with Lace 47
Puff Sleeves 48
Rugby Shirt 48
Rompers 52
Rompers with Waistband 54
Rompers with Front Zipper 55
Collar 56
Neckband 57
Panties 57
Panties with Lace 58

SECTION 5 JOGGING SUITS, SWEATSHIRTS,
CARDIGAN, PANTS,
SHORT PANTS 59
Sweatshirt 59
Hood 62
Lace and Ribbon 63
Drawstrings 64
Shirt with Side Closure 65
Shirt with Slit Opening 68
Cardigan Sweater 70
Pants 71
Short Pants 73
Panties with Lace 74

SECTION 6 BIB OVERALLS, BIB PANTS,
BIB SHORTS 75
Bib Overalls 75
Snaps at Inside Leg Seams 78
Eyelet Trim 79
Short Bib Overalls 80
Pockets 81
Bib Pants 82
Overlapped Bib 85

SECTION 7 JUMPSUITS, OVERALLS,
DRESSES 87
Jumpsuit 87
Leg Cuffs 90
Jumpsuit with Snaps 90
Jumpsuit with Neckband 91
Jumpsuit with Contrasting Top . . 92
Eyelet Trim 93
Overalls 94
Dresses 96
Basic Dress 96
Collar with Lace 100
Sleeve with Elastic in Casing . 100
Double Bodice 101
Neckline Ruffle 101
Tucks 102
Trims 103
Ruffles 103
Sundress 104
T-shirt Dress 107

SECTION 8 APPLIQUES, MONOGRAMS,
SLEEPING BAG 109
Appliques 109
Bunny Applique 111
Padded Applique 112
Outlining 112
Wall Hanging 113
Applique Designs 114
Sleeping Bag 119
Toy Bag 121
Monograms 122

YARDAGE REQUIREMENTS 124

MASTER PATTERN PIECES 126

SEWING FOR BABY is dedicated to you!
The new mothers, grandmothers and those of you
who have a special precious baby to sew for.

General Sewing Information

SECTION

1

Sewing for a baby is both fun and easy, but you must keep in mind that the design should be simple, the garment loose-fitting and the fabric easy to care for. Always be very careful to remove all pins when you try on the garment, or when it is finished. It is very easy to turn, say, a foot inside out and leave a pin inside. Also, when sewing on terry, the pins can be hidden in the fabric. When you have checked the garment for pins, check it again.

If you are constructing garments for a baby who is not yet born, use a color which can be used for either a boy or a girl, such as white, yellow or turquoise.

The most important thing is to choose the correct fabric. As a baby's skin is very tender, the first thing you should look for is a very soft fabric. You can use either a knit fabric or a woven fabric. The most suitable fiber for baby clothes is cotton.

You should wash baby clothes in hot water, especially when a baby is very small. Before washing, it is important to separate the garments by color. The white colors should be separated from the darks and pastels. White colors will have a tendency to turn grey if washed with colored fabrics. For baby clothes, try to pick a fabric that is colorfast, as one garment that runs could ruin an entire wash. If there are any stains on the clothes, these should be soaked in cold water before washing. This is important as hot water may cause the stains to set. All bedding for the baby, plus towels and washcloths, should be washed with the baby's clothes.

For the first couple of months of a baby's life, the baby clothes should be washed separately and not together with the rest of the family wash. The reason the baby's clothes should be washed in a special baby detergent is to help avoid rashes. You should also rinse the clothes an extra time so that you are sure all of the detergent is out of the clothes. If you are using cloth diapers, always wash them separately. Diaper stains are very difficult to remove, so you should rinse or flush the soiled diapers as soon as possible. Soak them in a pail of water until you are ready to wash them.

As any detergent left in the fabric may cause a rash, so will the sizing or finish in new fabrics. Therefore, always prewash the fabric in hot water. This will also preshrink the fabric at the same time. Preshrinking is important as almost all cotton shrinks to a certain extent.

While we recommend cotton for most of the baby's garments, there are also other fibers which may be used. For example, for a little sweater, booties and a bonnet, orlon may be used as orlon is very soft and it is ideal for these types of garments. Orlon looks like fine wool, but it is superior to wool when used for baby clothes as many small babies are allergic to wool, and it has a tendency to give them rashes.

You may also use combinations of cotton and synthetic fibers as long as they are soft. Nylon is a fiber which is very easy to care for; however, it is not suitable for small babies as the skin has to breathe and nylon does not absorb moisture. This again may have a tendency to produce rashes.

When the baby becomes more active and starts to crawl around, you will be able to use a much greater variety of fabrics such as corduroy, denim, permanent press, etc. As the baby gets older, the skin is not as sensitive.

Sweater fabric is available in a wide variety of fibers, designs and textures. For a baby, choose a very soft fabric, preferably orlon, as it is both soft and easy to care for. Some sweater fabric comes with one finished edge at the bottom. This ribbing is for the bottom of the sweater and the bottom of the sleeves. You can also find sweater fabric in the form of yardage. When you use sweater yardage, you must hem the sleeves and the bottom of the sweater. You may sew on special cuffs, or finish the bottom with a special trim. Stores which carry sweater fabric usually carry ribbing, which is used around the neck opening. This ribbing may also be used for the cuffs. If you are unable to obtain ribbing, you can use the sweater fabric, if you cut it across the grain.

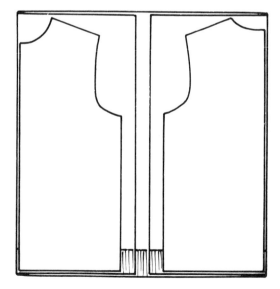

When you are using a fabric with a ribbed finish on the bottom, place the bottom of the pattern pieces, edge to edge, with the bottom of the ribbing.

The most common fabrics for babies' garments are single knit, stretch terry, interlock, stretch velour, and sweatshirt fleece. All of these fabrics are knits and are suitable for a variety of baby garments. However, it is important to check the pattern for the recommended fabrics and the recommended degree of stretch. Knits have different degrees of stretch; single knit, for example, has approximately 18% stretch while interlock or stretch terry has 25 to 35% stretch. If the pattern recommends stretch terry with 35% stretch and you use a single knit with 18% stretch, the garment would be too small.

To determine the correct amount of stretch, use the stretch chart below. Fold the fabric double and gently stretch the fabric on the crosswise grain. Do not stretch the fabric so tight that the fabric rolls excessively. This is also a good time to check the fabric for recovery. If the fabric does not go back to its original shape after being stretched, it will probably mean that the fabric will sag and stretch out of shape when the garment is worn.

Fabric with 18% stretch across the grain such as: Single knit, Double knit

4″ (10 cm) of Fabric should stretch

to at least here.

Fabric with 25% stretch across the grain such as: Interlock, Velour, Terry, Sweater fabric

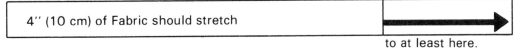

4″ (10 cm) of Fabric should stretch

to at least here.

Fabric with 35% stretch across the grain such as: Sweater fabric, Velour, Terry

4″ (10 cm) of Fabric should stretch

to at least here.

PATTERNS

In many areas, it is often very difficult to obtain patterns for all types of clothes for babies in the age group 0 to 18 months. Therefore, inside the back cover of this book, we have included Master Patterns to be used for a wide variety of garments. Some of the pattern pieces are interchangeable, so you can make a large variety of garments, using the same pattern pieces. How this is done is explained in the various sections. We will also explain how you can make minor changes in the design to obtain different effects. This will enable you, if you wish, to create your own designs.

All the Master Patterns have a ¼″ (6 mm) seam allowance included for all seams. This is the most common seam allowance used when sewing knit and stretch fabric. You can use this seam allowance for a regular sewing machine or a serger (overlock) machine.

Each Master Pattern includes four sizes: Small, Medium, Large and Extra Large. Choose pattern size by comparing the baby's height and weight to the measurement chart below.

Imperial Body Measurment Chart

Size	Small	Medium	Large	Extra Large
Month	0-3	3-6	6-12	12-18
Height	24"	26½"	29"	31½"
Weight	13 lb	18 lb	22 lb	26 lb

Metric Body Measurement Chart

Size	Small	Medium	Large	Extra Large
Month	0-3	3-6	6-12	12-18
Height	61 cm	67 cm	74 cm	80 cm
Weight	6 kg	8 kg	10 kg	12 kg

As babies vary greatly in weight and height, this must be taken into consideration when you are choosing the size of the pattern. If you make a sleeper in the small size, and the baby weighs only five pounds, do not be discouraged if it looks as if the baby is swimming in the garment. Babies grow very fast and you may be surprised to find that after one month the sleeper may be too small. For this reason, always make baby clothes larger than the actual size of the baby.

The weight of a baby approximately triples during the first year and the height increases close to 50% during this same period.

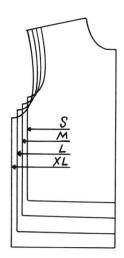

When you are constructing baby garments, do not hesitate to use the same pattern for both boys and girls as the patterns are the same. The illustration in the book may have a boy's outfit, but this pattern can be used if you are planning to sew for a girl. This applies to all baby patterns except girl's dresses.

The Master Patterns are printed on both sides of the paper. We recommend that you trace the pattern so that you can use the Master Pattern over and over again for all types of garments and for various sizes.

To trace the pattern, you can use tracing paper, but it is easier if you use a tracing cloth which is composed of pressed fibers. The cloth will last longer when you use the pattern over and over.

If you would like to have additional designs for babies which are not included in the Master Pattern, you can obtain additional KWIK • SEW patterns for babies at your local fabric store. KWIK • SEW patterns are carried by most leading fabric stores in the United States, Canada and Australia. If your store does not have the patterns, they can obtain them for you.

KWIK • SEW patterns have at least four sizes included in each envelope and each size is marked in a different color, making it very easy for you to cut out the correct size. Complete easy-to-follow instructions are included with each pattern as well as instructions on how to properly set your sewing machine so that you can sew correctly on all types of fabric.

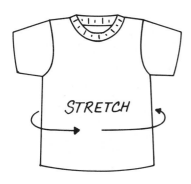

CUTTING

When cutting any type of fabric, it is very important to use a pair of sharp scissors so that you will obtain a clean cut. This is especially true if you are cutting stretch terry or a knitted fabric. Dull scissors have a tendency to chew the fabric rather than cut it. If they should become dull, get them sharpened as soon as possible. Never, we repeat, never use your sewing scissors for cutting anything else — especially paper! Cutting paper dulls the scissors very quickly.

When cutting out a garment using stretch fabric, you have to be sure that the stretch goes around the body. If you do not do this, you will end up with a garment that is long and narrow after it has been used a few times. This is especially true when you use loosely knitted fabric. If you are using two-way stretch fabric, the fabric will always stretch more in one direction than the other. Again, the greatest degree of stretch goes around the body.

Regardless of the fabric you are using, always be sure to follow the arrows on the pattern pieces to be sure you have the grain and stretch of the fabric in the right direction in order to insure a proper fit.

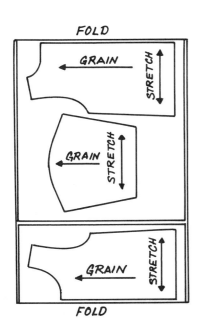

Before cutting out the fabric, the usual procedure is to place the fabric right side to right side. However, sometimes it is necessary to cut some of the pattern pieces out of a single thickness of fabric. In this way, you can often save on the amount of fabric you use. Before you cut out any of the pieces, place all the pattern pieces on the fabric and figure out how to proceed.

All Master Patterns have a ¼" (6 mm) seam allowance. If you wish to change the seam allowance, this should be taken into consideration before you start cutting.

If you are working with fabric that stretches, try to keep the fabric on top of the table and not hanging down as this will tend to pull it out of shape and the pieces will not be identical with the pattern.

There is a possibility, when working with fine kints, that you will have runs if a dull pin cuts the thread in a loop. Because of this, it is very important that you use very fine pins with ballpoints when you pin the pattern to the fabric. Some people prefer to use weights to hold the pattern pieces in place. Ash trays, cups, etc., will do very nicely as long as they keep the pattern steady on the fabric.

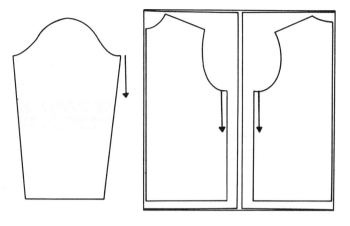

If you are using fabric that has a striped pattern, it is very important to line up the stripes before you start cutting. If you are constructing a garment and you are using a fabric with a design or a color design either throughout the fabric or only on parts of the fabric, you have to be more careful when you cut out the garment so that the design matches at the seams.

If the fabric has a design, measure the sleeve length first and cut out the sleeve. Measure the distance from the design to the underarm point; line up the back and front pattern pieces so that the distance from the design to the underarm point is exactly the same; then cut out the back and the front pieces.

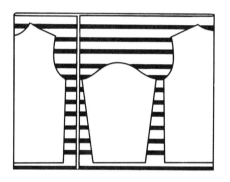

If you are constructing a shirt from striped fabric, be sure to match the stripes on the front, back and sleeves. When cutting out the shirt, place the underarm of the front, back and sleeves on the same stripe as illustrated.

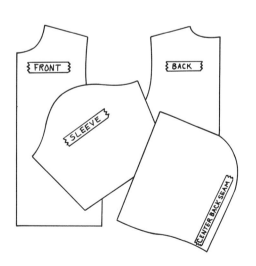

When you have cut out the pattern pieces, it is a good idea to mark each piece so that you do not mix them up. We recommend using transparent tape. This is the type of tape which you can sew through without the backing on the tape sticking to the needle. Place a small piece on the wrong side of the fabric, marking the side seams, back, etc. This tape has a dull finish which you can write on. Always use a pencil, as a ballpoint pen could spot the garment and these spots are very difficult to wash out.

This tape can also be used for basting and has many other useful applications. As you read on, you will find how this is done — plus you will discover many other shortcuts that rely on this tape. Be careful when you are using transparent tape on velour, stretch terry, or other fabric with a similar surface, as it may mark the fabric. Try the tape on a piece of scrap fabric before you use it.

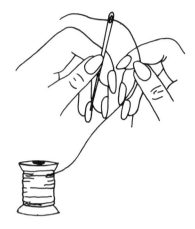

THREAD

The proper thread is very important when sewing. The basic rule to follow is to use cotton thread or cotton wrapped polyester thread on cotton fabric, and synthetic thread on synthetic fabric. As you will be washing the garments very often, it is important that you use a colorfast thread which will not shrink. Regardless of the type of thread you are using, always be sure to use the same thread on the top of the sewing machine as you use on the bobbin.

You may use the same thread on a serger (overlock) machine as you use on a standard sewing machine. It is more economical to purchase large spools of thread which are available in cones in all the basic colors. If you are using cones of synthetic thread such as nylon, cover the cones with nylon netting to prevent the thread from unraveling. When you are using a serger (overlock) machine, you will always run out of looper threads first as these use more thread. Switch the needle spool with the loopers when you are getting low on thread.

Almost all functions, when sewing baby clothes, can be done on a sewing machine. However, in some cases, you may have to sew a few stitches by hand, and the following should always be kept in mind if you are using synthetic thread. All synthetic thread is manufactured from synthetic fibers and these fibers tend to revert to their original shape. It is very important, when sewing by hand, that you always thread the needle from the end coming off the spool. If you do not follow this procedure, you will end up with small knots and fraying in the thread.

CORRECT TENSION

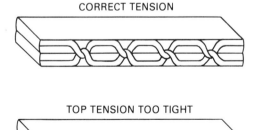

TOP TENSION TOO TIGHT

BOTTOM TENSION TOO TIGHT

SEWING

Before you start sewing, take a small piece of scrap fabric, double the fabric, and sew a straight stitch. Check the stitches to be sure the tensions are correct. The perfect thread tension results when the top and bottom tensions are exactly equal and the knot is buried in the fabric and cannot be seen. The best rule to follow is to adjust the tensions so that the stitch appears the same on both sides. The diagrams on this page show you how to adjust for the correct tension. Try to adjust only the top tension as this is easier to do on all sewing machines, but in some cases you may have to adjust both the top and bottom tensions.

If you are using a serger (overlock) machine, refer to the instruction book for your machine for instructions on how to adjust the tension.

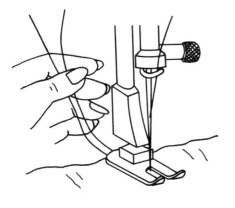

If you are using a regular sewing machine, and as most of the fabric you will be using for baby clothes is very soft, you will find it much easier to start a seam if you lower the needle into the fabric and hold both the top and bottom threads in your hand behind the presser foot. As the machine starts to sew, slowly pull these threads toward the rear of the machine. This will help the machine feed the material and eliminate the tendency of the material to bunch up under the presser foot.

If your sewing machine has a tendency to skip stitches, this is usually caused by a dull or bent needle. The first thing you should do is to change the needle. We recommend using a fine needle 10/70 or 12/80.

If your machine continues to skip stitches and you are sewing on knit fabrics, we recommend that you use a ballpoint needle. This type of needle has a slightly rounded point, and as a result, it tends to go between the fabric yarns rather than piercing the yarn and causing it to split or break.

It is also very important to use the correct pressure on the presser foot. Most of the up-to-date machines can be adjusted, which is usually simple to do. For woven and non-stretch fabric, you should use normal pressure on the presser foot. For loosely knitted and very stretchy fabric, you should loosen the pressure slightly on the presser foot.

When you are sewing terrycloth, stretch terry, or any other fabric with a similar surface, it is sometimes difficult to sew the seam using the regular presser foot. The loops in the fabric get caught in the slot on the foot, and the fabric bunches up under the presser foot. A roller presser foot will eliminate this problem. The foot rolls over the fabric, and you never have to worry that the fabric will bunch up under the roller presser foot.

SEAMS

For a very small baby, it is very important to have soft seams. The stitch you use should vary according to the type of fabric you are using. The type of sewing machine you are using will also be a factor in determining what kind of stitch you will use.

STRAIGHT STITCH MACHINE

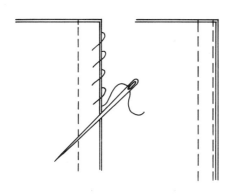

When you are using a ¼" (6 mm) seam allowance in non-stretch fabric, sew the seam using medium stitch length. Overcast the edges by hand if the fabric has a tendency to unravel, or stitch the seam allowance together close to the raw edges.

When sewing on stretch fabric, stretch the fabric in back as well as in front of the presser foot as you sew the seams. We suggest that you sew the seam twice for greater strength. To prevent unraveling, overcast the edges by hand, or stitch the seam allowances together close to the raw edge.

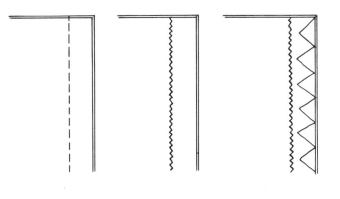

ZIGZAG MACHINE

When you are using a ¼" (6 mm) seam allowance in non-stretch fabric, sew the seam using a medium length straight stitch. Overcast the raw edges together by using a zigzag stitch.

For stretch fabric, sew the seam using a narrow zigzag stitch. This will give you a strong seam with a certain degree of stretch. If the fabric has a tendency to unravel, overcast the edges with a large zigzag stitch.

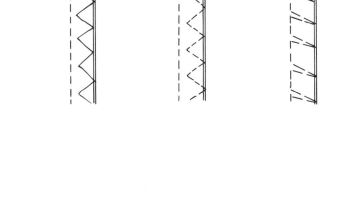

REVERSE CYCLE MACHINE

When sewing on non-stretch fabric using a ¼" (6 mm) seam allowance, sew the seam with a medium length straight stitch, overcast the edges together with a zigzag stitch, or you can use a three-step zigzag stitch. On certain types of fabric, you can use an overlock stitch to sew the seam and overcast in one operation. This saves you a great amount of time, as you do not have to sew the seam twice.

When sewing on any type of stretch fabric, we recommend using an overlock stitch. This makes the seam both strong and elastic.

To get a smooth, soft seam when you are sewing terrycloth, sew the seam with a straight stitch, open the seam allowance, and sew down the edges of the seam allowance with a three-step zigzag. This is a stitch where the machine sews three stitches on each zig and each zag. This stitch is almost invisible on the right side.

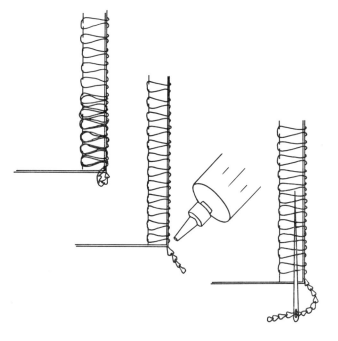

SERGER (OVERLOCK) MACHINE

This type of sewing machine gives a very professional look. In addition, the seams will withstand many repeated washings. Serger (overlock) machines sew, overcast and trim the excess seam allowance in one step. When using a serger (overlock) machine, be sure that you are using the correct seam allowance so that the garment will fit properly. Try the seam on a scrap piece of fabric and mark the location for the edge of the fabric. Guide the edge of the fabric along this line.

If it is necessary to lock the seams at the ends, use any of the following methods:

1. Sew a chain, then turn the fabric and sew for about ¼" (6 mm).

2. Use "Fray Check"® which glues the threads together.

3. Sew a chain and insert the chain through the seam with a large needle or crochet hook.

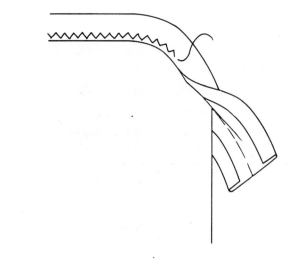

BIAS TAPE

A very easy way to finish the raw edges on many baby garments is to use bias tape. Bias tape is available in various widths with either a single or double fold. The single fold tape is flat with folds on the outside and the raw edges together at the center of the tape. This type of tape should be folded once more, double, wrong side to wrong side to hide the raw edges. This is already done when you use double folded bias tape.

The easiest way to finish off raw edges of the fabric is to insert the raw edges of the fabric into the fold of the bias tape and sew close to the inner edge of the tape. Be sure to catch the tape on the wrong side. The easiest way to do this is to use a narrow zigzag stitch.

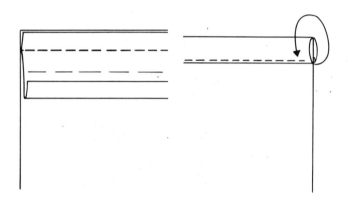

Another way to finish raw edges using bias tape is to unfold one side of the tape and place the right side of the tape on the wrong side of the garment with the raw edges of the tape, matching the raw edges of the fabric. Sew a seam on the fold of the tape. Now fold the tape over the seam allowance to the right side. Topstitch from the right side close to the edge of the tape.

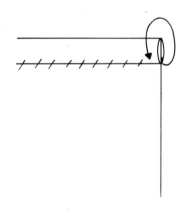

If you prefer not to have any seams showing on the right side, sew on the bias tape by placing the tape on the right side, raw edges together. Sew on the tape, fold the tape over the raw edges to the wrong side, and stitch in place by hand.

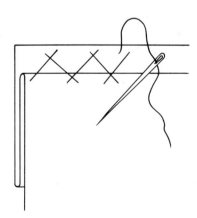

HEMMING

The most common way to hem baby clothes is simply to fold the hem to the wrong side and topstitch the hem with either a straight stitch, a small zigzag, or a three-step zigzag stitch. If you want an invisible hem, for example, on a little girl's dress, do it either by hand or use a blind hem stitch. This stitch will be invisible on the right side.

PRESSING

It is very important to press the seams as you sew them; this is especially true for children's clothes which are small and it is extremely difficult to reach into the garment to press the seams after they have been finished.

It is also very important to use the correct type of iron and set the temperature recommended for the fabric you are using. If you are not sure of the content of the fabric, always use a cooler setting so that you are on the safe side.

A steam iron gives much better results when working with knit and stretch fabric. This is especially true when pressing sweater fabric. The steam does the work in shaping the garment.

The difference between ironing and pressing is that ironing is running the iron over the fabric in long back and forth strokes using pressure to remove creases and wrinkles in the fabric. Pressing is a press-lift, press-lift motion. You are applying both steam and heat to gently form the garment. When working with sweater fabric, the iron should actually not touch the fabric. The heat and steam do the work.

A pressing ham is very helpful, especially for form pressing the neckline on sweaters and T-shirts.

Before you cut out the fabric, be sure to press out the creases. Again, make sure that your iron is set for the correct temperature. Sometimes you will find fabric that has a crease which you cannot remove. In this case, make sure when you cut out the pattern that this crease ends up in an inconspicuous place.

When you are making a seam using ¼" (6 mm) seam allowance, first press the seam flat in the same grain direction as it was sewn. Then, press the seam allowance toward one side.

Even when using a larger seam allowance, always press the seam flat and then press the seam allowance open.

Female

Male

SNAPS

You will use many snaps on baby garments. Snaps make it much easier to change the baby. Because you will be using so many snaps, we suggest that you buy a plier kit for snaps. This will save you a lot of time and make it much easier to attach the snaps. Make sure that you apply the snaps at the correct position, as it is almost impossible to change them. Remember that girl's clothing closes from the right, and boy's from the left. When you are using snaps, be very careful that all of the points of the prongs are enclosed in the ring. These points are very sharp, and if one is sticking out, it could scratch the baby.

We recommend that you use interfacing under the snaps as the fabric is very soft and this will stabilize the fabric. The easiest method is to use press-on interfacing.

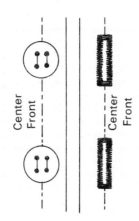

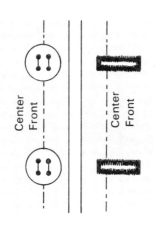

BUTTONS AND BUTTONHOLES

Before making a buttonhole, check the instruction book for your sewing machine as the procedure is different for different sewing machines. When you mark your buttonholes, we suggest that you make the buttonhole ⅛" (2 mm) larger than the button. You can use either horizontal or vertical buttonholes. If you are making vertical buttonholes, you make the buttonhole on the center front or center back line. If you are making horizontal buttonholes, start the buttonhole ⅛" (2 mm) from the center front or center back line toward the edge of the garment. Sew on the buttons on the center front or center back line of the other piece. By following this procedure, the buttons will always end up at the center front or center back.

When you cut open the buttonholes, it is a good idea to place a pin at the end of the buttonhole at cross angles to the buttonhole. This will prevent you from cutting too large a hole, and perhaps ruining the garment.

Buttons can be sewn on either by machine or by hand. If you are using a machine, drop your feed dogs; set the machine for zigzag. The width of the stitch should be the same as the distance between the holes in the buttons. Again, refer to your sewing machine instruction book.

At The Very Beginning . . .

SECTION 2

Every mother-to-be, expecting her first baby, usually receives varied advice from friends and relatives on what and how much her baby will need. There are certain basic items which you should have such as crib sheets, receiving blankets, bath towels, wash cloths, shirts, sleepers and diapers. How many of each item you will need depends upon how often you plan to wash. If you have a washer and dryer at home, you will need less than if you wash a couple of times a week. As a general rule, when the baby comes home from the hospital, the baby will have to be fed every four hours. Each feeding, more often than not, necessitates a complete change of clothing. It is amazing how often the new baby will spit up or wet through the diapers. As far as wetting through, boys are a greater problem than girls.

Normally, you will be using a form-fitted sheet on the crib. As this type of sheet is more difficult to change, place a pad underneath the sheet; on top of the sheet place another smaller pad; on top of the pad, a receiving blanket. Now, all you have to do is wash the receiving blanket and the small pad. This will apply for the first three months when the baby is not apt to move around as much. This means you will need fewer crib sheets, but more receiving blankets. The following are our suggestions for minimum quantities, but again, these will vary according to how often you wash and with the climate.

    2-3 crib sheets
    6-8 receiving blankets
    2 soft bath towels
    3-4 wash cloths
    6 shirts
    6 sleepers (usually not needed in a hot climate)
    1-2 blankets
    supply of diapers

Do not count on receiving these as shower gifts. Probably the most common items you will receive will be a fancy sweater with pretty booties, silver spoons and banks, or baby mugs and plates. All of these are nice to have, but they are not really necessary. What is necessary are more crib sheets, receiving blankets, etc. The more of these items you have on hand, the less often you will have to wash, and therefore, the less work you will have to do. This is important, as feeding and changing the baby every four hours will keep you busy.

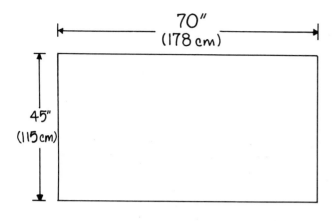

CRIB SHEET

A crib sheet is easy to sew. We suggest that you use a very soft cotton knit fabric. Remember to prewash the fabric in order to shrink it and at the same time, remove the sizing. You need a piece of fabric 45". (115 cm) wide and 70" (178 cm) long. The most stretch should go across the crib.

This fits a standard American 6-year crib which is 28" x 52" (71 cm x 132 cm).

If you plan to use another size mattress, measure the mattress length and width. Add 3" (8 cm) plus the thickness of the mattress to all four sides.

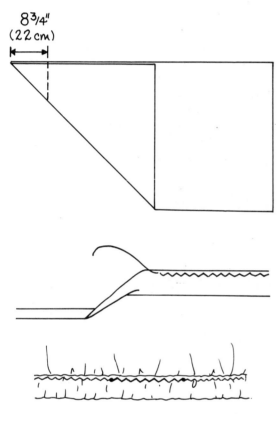

Fold each corner in half, right side to right side. On the raw edge, measure from the point 8¾" (22 cm). From this point, sew a seam across to the folded edge. Cut off the excess fabric.

The easiest way to finish the sheet is to use elastic all the way around the sheet. Fold under the raw edge ¾" (2 cm) and press. Fold under the raw edge ¼" (6 mm) and sew a seam as close as possible to the inside edge. The best stitch to use is a narrow zigzag stitch. Sew the seam completely around, leaving an opening to insert the elastic.

Cut a piece of ⅜" (1 cm) wide elastic 90" (228 cm) long. Insert the elastic inside the casing. Overlap the two ends of the elastic and secure by sewing across a few times. Close the opening.

Another easy way to finish a sheet is to overcast the edges with a serger (overlock) machine. Sew the elastic on the wrong side with the edge of the elastic even with the edge of the fabric and stretch the elastic around the sheet as you sew.

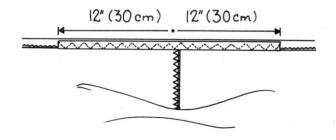

You may want to hem the sheet and apply the elastic only to the corners. Cut four lengths of elastic 15" (38 cm) long. Mark the sheet 12" (30 cm) in from each corner. Place the elastic on the hem on the wrong side. Stretch the elastic between the marks and sew on the elastic. Use either a zigzag or a three-step zigzag stitch.

RECEIVING BLANKET

You can make a receiving blanket using soft synthetic fabric or soft woven or knit cotton. The advantage of using cotton is that you can wash it along with the other cotton items such as shirts, sheets, etc. Synthetic fabrics usually have to be washed and dried using a lower temperature.

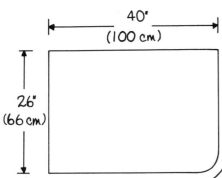

Cut a piece of fabric 40" (100 cm) long and 26" (66 cm) wide. Cut off the square corners so that they are slightly rounded. This will make it easier to hem the blanket.

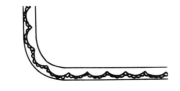

Hem the blanket, using one of the following methods:

- Turn a narrow hem to the wrong side and sew completely around.

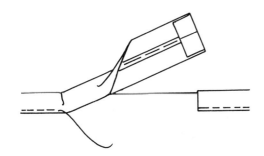

- Turn a hem once to the wrong side and sew a decorative stitch, using a contrasting thread. Trim off the excess fabric close to the stitches. This will give you a very attractive edge.

- To apply bias tape around the blanket, insert the raw edge into the tape. Topstitch through all the layers all the way around. Finish the ends by folding them under.

- If you are using a serger (overlock) machine, sew the seam all around. This can be very attractive if you are using thread of contrasting color.

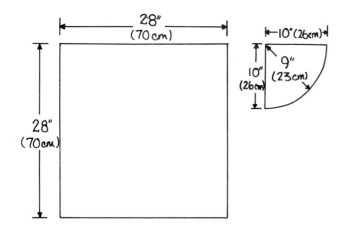

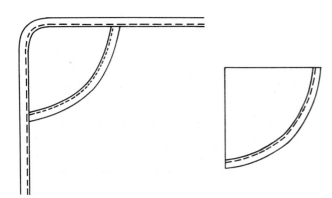

If you are using very lightweight fabric for the blanket, we suggest that you use two thicknesses of fabric. Cut two pieces for the blanket. Place the two pieces, right side to right side, and sew around the blanket, leaving an opening for turning. Turn the blanket inside out and close the opening. You can either topstitch around close to the edges or use a decorative stitch.

BATH TOWEL WITH HOOD

When you have given the baby a bath, it is very important to cover up the baby quickly, so the baby does not get chilled. A bath towel with a hood is easy to make and is very practical.

We suggest that you use soft terrycloth. Cut a square piece of fabric 28" (70 cm). Cut another piece for the hood in a triangular shape as illustrated.

It is not necessary to make the towel square. You may want to round off one or all of the corners.

Finish all of the raw edges with bias tape or any other suitable binding. Press the binding lengthwise, wrong side to wrong side. Start on the curved edge of the hood by inserting the raw edge into the tape. Make sure that you catch the tape on both sides of the material as you are sewing.

Pin the triangle on one corner of the fabric. Now, sew the tape all the way around the square, at the same time attaching the hood to the square. The towel is now completed.

You may want to add an applique to one corner to give the towel a more personalized look. See Section 8 for Appliques. If you want a simple bath towel, just eliminate the hood.

WASH CLOTH

Use the same fabric as you used for the towel. Cut a piece approximately 8" (20 cm) by 10" (26 cm). Finish the raw edges using bias tape as previously described or overlock the edges.

BIBS

Regardless of the size of the bib, the technique for making them is the same. You will want a small bib when the baby starts teething. So that it does not look so much like a bib, use the same fabric as the outfit the baby is wearing. This is an excellent way to use up small pieces of scrap fabric. You can also dress up any style bib with the use of appliques (see Section 8). The most practical bibs are the ones lined with plastic. As plastic does not shrink when washed, it is very important to preshrink the fabric and the bias tape in order to keep the bib from curling up.

For a teething bib, cut a piece of fabric approximately 7" x 7" (18 cm x 18 cm). Fold the fabric double and cut the edges as illustrated for a rounded bib. Use soft plastic for the lining and cut it in the same shape.

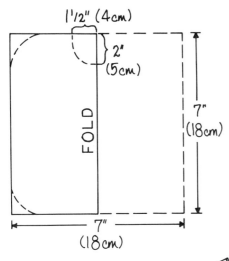

Sew the plastic and fabric together by sewing around the raw edges. Do **not** use pins, as they will make holes in the plastic.

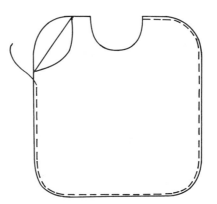

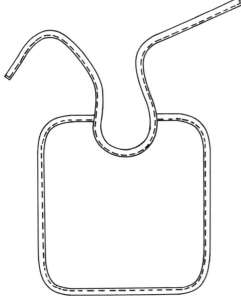

Finish the outside edge with bias tape. Use a piece of bias tape for the neck and for the tie bands. This bias tape should be approximately 20" (50 cm) long. Mark the center front. Divide the bias tape in half and mark. Insert the raw edges of the bib into the tape, matching marks. Sew the bias tape together, starting at one end and continue around the neckline to the other end of the tape.

A pretty teething bib for a little girl can easily be made with the addition of ruffled lace on the outer edge. Use either pregathered lace or cut a strip of regular lace twice the length of the outer edge of the bib. Sew gathering stitches on the lace and pull the thread until the length of the lace is equal to the outside edge of the bib. Place the straight edge of the lace on the right side of the bib, raw edges together. Sew on the lace all the way around.

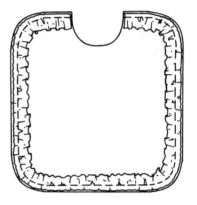

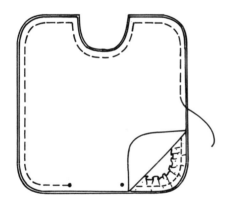

Place the lining or plastic, right side to right side, over the lace. Sew around the outside edge and the neck, leaving an opening so that you can turn the bib right side out.

Topstitch completely around the bib. Attach a tie band on each side of the neck opening.

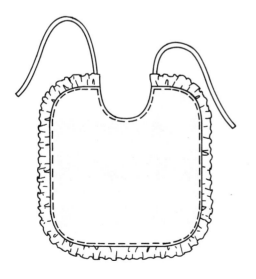

26

Lightweight terrycloth makes a very practical bib to use when the baby is eating. Cut a piece of fabric approximately 9½" x 12" (24 cm x 30 cm). Fold the fabric double, lengthwise, and cut out as illustrated.

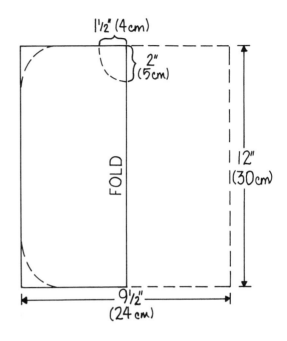

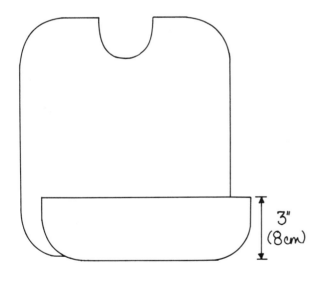

If you would like to have a pocket at the bottom of the bib, cut the pocket the same shape as the bottom of the bib 3" (8 cm) high.

Line the pocket with plastic and finish the top edge with bias tape. Sew the bib using the same procedure as used for the teething bib.

Instead of using bias tape around the bib, you can finish the edge with an overlock stitch on the serger (overlock) machine.

If you plan to use an applique on any bib, sew on the appliques **before** you line the bib.

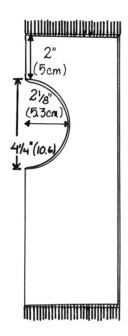

BIB MADE FROM A GUEST TOWEL

Fold a pretty guest towel in half and cut out a 2⅛" (5.3 cm) circle 2" (5 cm) from one side. For the neckband, cut a piece of ribbing 2½" (6.5 cm) wide and 9½" (24 cm) long. Sew the neckband into a circle.

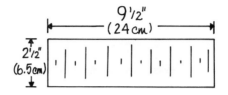 

Fold the neckband double lengthwise, wrong sides together. Divide the neckband and the neck opening into fourths with pins.

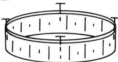

Pin the neckband to the neck opening with the right sides and raw edges together, matching the pins and the seam on the band to the center back. Sew around the opening, stretching, the band to fit the opening.

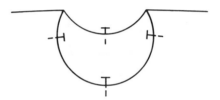

BUMPER PADS

A bumper pad may not be necessary when the baby is very small and does not move or roll over as it sleeps. However, when the baby grows a little larger, it will roll and toss, and this is when you need the bumper pad so the baby will not hurt itself against the sides of the crib. A bumper pad may be very plain but if you have a little extra time, you can really do wonders to the pad by the use of appliques, or you can finish the top edges with laces or ruffles.

A bumper pad can be any length, but the size we are giving will fit most standard size cribs. The finished length of the pad is 162" (411 cm) long. The pad can be any width but the most common is between 8" to 12" (20 cm to 30.5 cm). The bumper pads may be constructed using one color fabric, or you may want to use one color for the inside and another color for the outside. You can use one length of fabric for the entire pad, but it is more economical to use four pieces. Cut four pieces for each side of the pad 41½" (106 cm) long and 10" (25 cm) wide.

Sew the four pieces together for both sides. You will end up with two long pieces; use ½" (1.3 cm) seam allowances.

On the piece you plan to use for the inside of the pad, you will have to sew across to keep the padding in place. Therefore, divide each section in thirds and mark these lines.

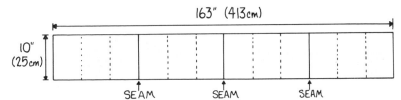

Cut one length of batting 163" (413 cm) long and 10" (25 cm) wide. Piece the batting together if it is not long enough.

Place the fabric pieces, wrong sides together, with the batting in between. Pin them together at the bottom and the top edges. Sew close to the edges. Sew across the marked stitching lines.

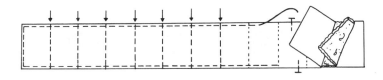

For the tie bands, cut nine pieces of double fold bias tape each 20" (51 cm) long. Sew the folded tape edges together. Fold each piece in half and pin as illustrated. Sew across each piece of tape to keep them in place.

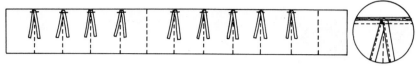

Finish the top and the bottom edges of the bumper pad with wide bias tape. Fold the bias tape in half, lengthwise, and press. Insert the raw edges of the bumper pad into the fold of the tape and pin in place. Sew through all layers — be sure to catch the tape on the wrong side.

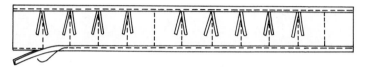

Finish the short ends of the bumper pad in the same manner, but be sure to leave 10" (25 cm) on each end for ties. Sew the edges of the ties together as illustrated.

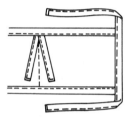

A pretty variation may be made by adding a ruffle or pregathered eyelet. Cut out the bumper pad as explained previously. Sew the sections together.

Pin the ruffle to the top edge of the fabric to be used for the inside. The ruffle should face down. Sew on the ruffle.

Position the tie band as previously described. Sew on the ties over the ruffle.

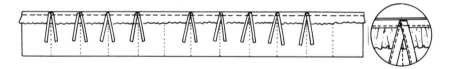

Place the batting on the wrong side of the other piece, baste it to keep it in place. Pin the two fabric pieces together, right side to right side, and sew the top edge.

Turn the pad right side out. Baste the ends and the bottom edge together. Finish the bottom edge and the ends, using bias tape as previously described.

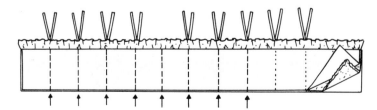

COMFORTER

A very attractive comforter for the crib can be made in a very short time. The measurements given are for a comforter 30" x 50" (76 cm x 127 cm). Both sides of the comforter can be made from one color fabric, or you can use a contrasting color on the other side. We suggest that you use a lightweight cotton on one side and a lightweight flannel on the other side. Cut two pieces of fabric 31" x 51" (79 cm x 130 cm). Cut a piece of batting the same size. The thickness of the batting will depend upon how warm you want the comforter to be.

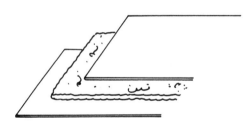

You can finish the edges of the comforter with or without bias tape. If you use bias tape, you can use tape the same color as the comforter or you may prefer a contrasting color. When you are using bias tape to finish the edges, place the two layers of fabric, wrong sides together, with the batting in between. Baste the three layers, all around the comforter, close to the edges to keep the three layers in place.

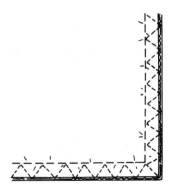

Trim the outside edges so they are even. To make it easier to apply the bias tape, we recommend that you overcast the edges. Here is a good opportunity to use a serger (overlock) machine as it trims and overcasts in one operation.

Use a wide bias tape to finish the raw edges of the comforter as described in Section 1.

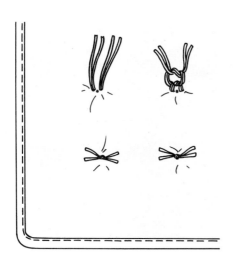

To keep the layers together and to keep the batting from shifting, make twelve marks an equal distance apart on the top layer. At the twelve marks, make ties using yarn. Four-ply knitting yarn works well, or you can use embroidery floss. Use a large-eyed crewel needle; the yarn can be single or double. On the marks, take a stitch down through all three layers; now, stitch back up. Tie the ends of the yarn with a square knot. Cut the ends of the yarn so that they are 1" (2.5 cm) long.

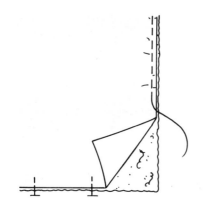

If you do not want to use bias tape around the comforter, place the batting on the wrong side of one layer of fabric and pin in place. Sew close to the edges.

Pin the other piece of fabric, right side to right side, and sew all the way around, leaving a 14" (35 cm) opening for turning. Turn the comforter right side out. Close the opening. Tie the comforter as described previously.

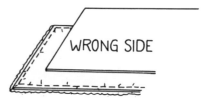

If you would like to have eyelet trim around the outer edges of the comforter, use the pregathered eyelet. Sew on the eyelet using the same procedures as described on page 26.

If you would like to decorate the comforter with an applique, be sure to apply the applique to the top BEFORE you sew the comforter together. The comforter can be tied or you can quilt around the outside edges of the applique using hand stitches.

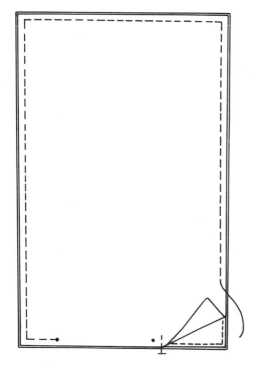

Sleepers
Kimonos

Since the first few months of a baby's life are spent mostly sleeping, adequate sleepers are the most important items in the wardrobe. The first tiny sleepers are outgrown very quickly and must soon be replaced with larger ones.

When babies are sleeping, they tend to move around a lot. Therefore, sleepwear should be comfortable and also loose-fitting. They should be warm and cozy, and the weight of the fabric used will vary according to how warm you keep the sleeping room.

We recommend using stretch fabric with a 25% stretch across the grain such as stretch terry or interlock. These fabrics are available in different weights from light to medium weight. Compare the fabric to the stretch chart in Section 1. This is necessary to insure proper fit. Be sure the greatest amount of stretch goes around the body. For the neckband and the sleeve bands, use ribbing cut across the grain.

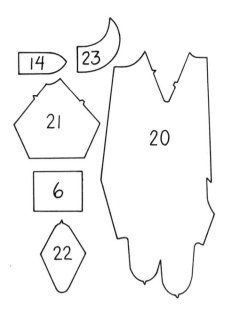

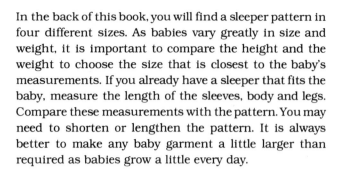

In the back of this book, you will find a sleeper pattern in four different sizes. As babies vary greatly in size and weight, it is important to compare the height and the weight to choose the size that is closest to the baby's measurements. If you already have a sleeper that fits the baby, measure the length of the sleeves, body and legs. Compare these measurements with the pattern. You may need to shorten or lengthen the pattern. It is always better to make any baby garment a little larger than required as babies grow a little every day.

Use Master patterns:
20 - Sleeper	6 - Sleeve Cuff
21 - Sleeves	23 - Collar, or
22 - Crotch piece	14 - Neckband

Place the fabric double, right side to right side, and cut out the patterns with the center back on the fold. Be certain to follow the arrows for the correct grain and stretch of the fabric. A ¼" (6 mm) seam allowance is included for all seams on the sleeper.

If you want to make a monogram or sew on an applique, it is easier to do this before you construct the sleeper. How this is done is explained in Section 8.

Start by sewing the sleeve seams. It is easier to sew on the cuffs before you construct the sleeper. The cuffs are made from ribbing.

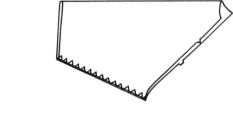

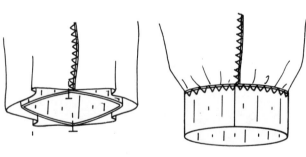

Sew the ends of the cuffs, right side to right side, to form circles. Fold each cuff lengthwise, wrong sides together.

Divide the cuffs and the sleeve openings in half with pins.

Pin the cuffs to the right side of the sleeve openings, matching pins and raw edges. Sew on the cuffs, stretching the cuffs to fit the sleeve openings.

A quick way to sew on the cuff is to place the cuff, right side to right side, and sew on the cuff before you sew the sleeve seam. Sew the sleeve seam and the cuff in one operation.

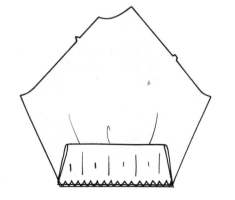

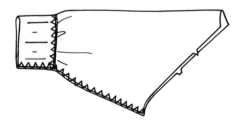

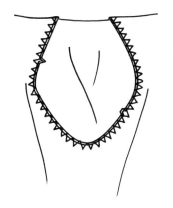

Sew on the sleeve to front and back raglan seams. Sew in one operation, matching the notches.

You can use either a neckband made from ribbing, or you can finish the neck opening with a collar.

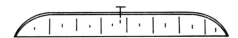

NECKBAND

If you plan to use a neckband (Master pattern 14), fold the neckband lengthwise, wrong sides together, on the folding line and press. As ribbing has a tendency to stretch when you press it, recheck the piece against the pattern and trim off any excess. Mark the center back of the neckband with a pin.

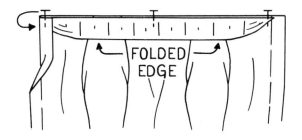

Pin the neckband to the neck opening, right side to right side, with the raw edges together. Match the pin to the center back and the ends of the band to the front (folding line). Fold the front facing on the folding line to the right side over the neckband. Sew the band to the neck opening, stretching the band to fit the neck opening, including the facing in the seam. Turn the facing to the wrong side.

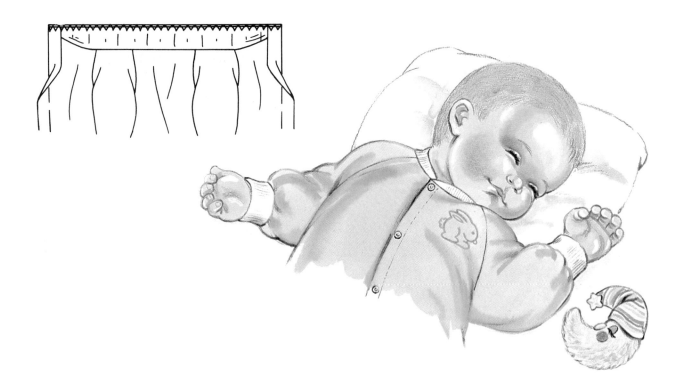

COLLAR

If you plan to use a collar (Master pattern 23) instead of a neckband, place the collars right side to right side, and sew around the outer edge, leaving the neckline open. Turn the collar right side out.

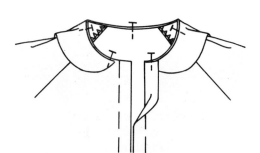

Mark the center back of the neckline. Pin the collar on the right side of the neckline, matching the center back with the ends of the collar ⅜" (1 cm) from the folding line.

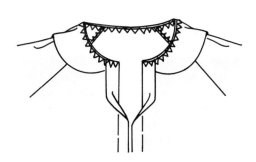

Fold the front facing on the folding line to the right side over the collar. Sew on the collar through all layers, including the facing in the seam. Ease the neckline to fit the collar. Turn the front facing to the wrong side.

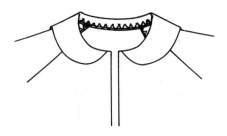

If you have a serger, and you would like to have a variation on the outside edge of the collar, place the collar pieces, wrong side to wrong side, and trim away the ¼" (6 mm) seam allowance on the outer edge. Sew around the outer edge using either the same color thread or a contrasting color for a special effect. Sew on the collar as previously described.

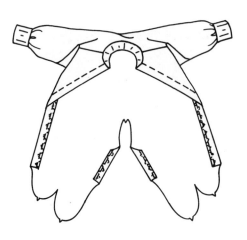

Overcast both front edges of the sleeper. Fold both fronts on the folding line, to the wrong side, and sew close to the overcasted edge to hold down the front facing.

Overcast the facing on the back inside leg seam. Fold the facing on the folding line to the wrong side, and sew a seam close to the overcasted edge.

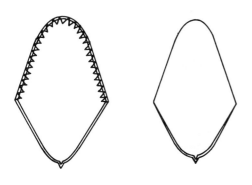

Place the crotch pieces right side to right side. Sew around the front part of the crotch, leaving the back part (notched side) open. Turn the crotch piece right side out.

Pin the crotch piece to the back, right sides and raw edges together, matching the notch to the center back and with the edges of the crotch piece even with the edges of the inside leg seams. Sew the crotch piece in place.

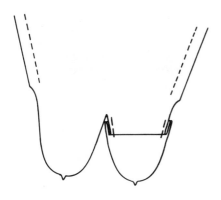

To make the foot, pin a tuck between the marks on the bottom of the back leg. This becomes the heel for the foot. Sew the tuck in place close to the edges.

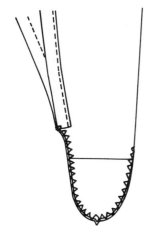

Place each leg, right side to right side, and sew around the foot as illustrated. Turn the feet right side out.

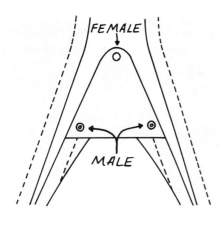

SNAPS

The parts of a snap are usually referred to as being either "male" or "female". We are using these terms as it makes it easier to explain the placement of the snaps. Refer to Section 1.

Start applying the snaps to the crotch piece, following the illustration.

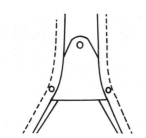

Apply the female part of the snaps to match the male part. Snap together.

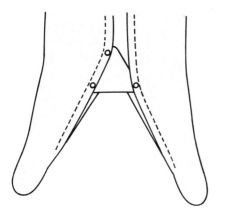

Overlap the right front edge over the crotch piece and apply the male part of the snap to match the female part at the top of the crotch piece.

⅝" (1.5 cm) below this snap, apply a male part. Divide the remaining distance of the right front equally and apply the male part of the snaps.

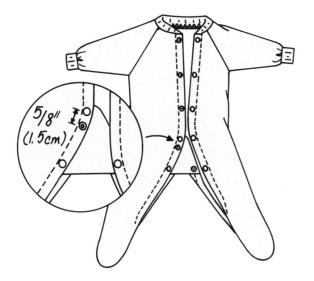

Overlap the left front and mark the placement for the snap, and apply female part.

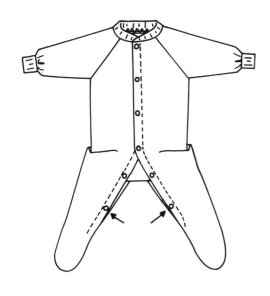

Apply the snaps to the inside leg seams, one or two depending on the size of the sleeper.

KIMONO

For a newborn baby, you may want to use a kimono, a sleeper without legs. We recommend a single knit or interlock fabric.

Use Master patterns:
- 20 - Sleeper
- 21 - Sleeves
- 14 - Neckband
- 6 - Cuffs (optional)

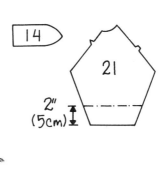

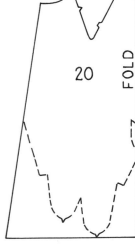

If you make the kimono **without** cuffs, you have to add the necessary length to the bottom of the sleeve; adding about 2" (5 cm) should be sufficient.

On Master pattern 20, change the pattern by extending the center back line and the front line down to the bottom of the toe (see illustration).

Cut out the pattern by placing the center back on a fold. The construction for the sleeves and the neck is the same as used for a sleeper.

If you are not using the cuffs, overcast the bottom edge of the sleeves, and turn ½" (1.3 cm) to the wrong side for a hem. Sew a seam close to the overcasted edge.

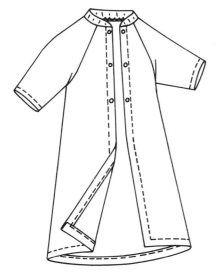

This type of garment can either be open at the bottom, or it can have a casing with a drawstring at the bottom. If you are constructing a kimono which will open at the bottom and front, at the center front, fold under the front facing ¾" (2 cm) to the wrong side, and hem. Apply about three snaps from the neck down, leaving the rest open.

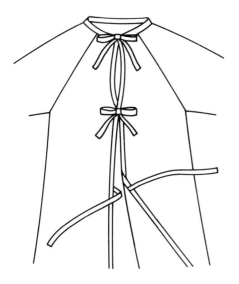

Or, if you want, finish the center front using bias tape (see Section 1 for applying bias tape). First, be sure to cut away the front facing. Bias tape can also be used around the neck opening instead of a neckband. On a kimono you can make ties to close the front instead of using snaps. Hem the bottom edge.

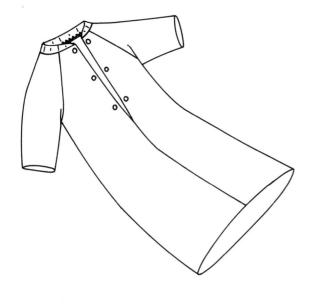

If you are using a drawstring at the bottom of a kimono, sew the center front seam, leaving enough of an opening at the top so that the baby easily slips into the kimono. Use either snaps or tie bands to close the front opening.

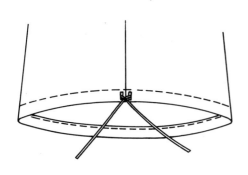

At the bottom, fold a 1" (2.5 cm) hem to the wrong side. Sew a seam close to the edge, leaving a 1" (2.5 cm) opening. Insert a band or string through the casing so that you can close the bottom opening.

T-shirts
Rompers
Panties

T-shirts are probably the most versatile and practical garments in a baby's wardrobe. Teamed with overalls, playsuits, shorts or pants, they complete an outfit. They can be adapted to any season of the year by using long or short sleeves. Fortunately, a T-shirt is one of the simplest garments to make. You can use a wide variety of colors and fabric designs. Numerous attractive ensembles can be created by using different or contrasting colors for the sleeves and neckband. Appliques or monograms on a T-shirt will give it an interesting and personal effect.

For the cuffs and the neckband, we recommend using ribbing. For the T-shirt itself, single knit is the best fabric to use. Single knits can range from a very smooth texture to those which have a textured finish.

Single knit usually comes approximately 60" (152 cm) wide. This fabric tends to roll at the edges, it is sometimes doubled and the edges are knitted or sewn together at the mill. This makes it easier for the manufacturer and the fabric stores to handle the rolls or bolts. Some single knit is knitted in a tubular shape. It is often difficult to see where the edges are joined. In some instances, it looks like a flaw. This is where you should cut the material apart before proceeding. This will eliminate the possiblility of ending up with this seam or flaw in the front or back, etc., where it will be very noticeable.

If you are not certain of the content, or if you do not know the shrinkage factor, we recommend, to be on the safe side, to pre-shrink in hot water before proceeding. Cotton knit should always be preshrunk.

You should also be careful when cutting out the garment that the crease in the fabric is not in a conspicuous place, as this crease is very often difficult to press out.

A small baby has a head which is large compared to the size of its body, and no baby likes to have anything tight pulled over its head. Therefore, we suggest that you use snaps on both shoulders. However, if you only want snaps on one side, this is explained later in this section.

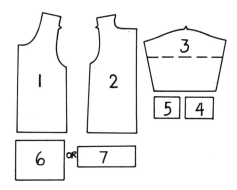

T-SHIRT WITH SET-IN SLEEVES

Use Master patterns:
1 - Front
2 - Back
3 - Sleeves
4 - Front Neckband
5 - Back Neckband
6 - Long Sleeve Cuff, or
7 - Short Sleeveband

For the neckband and cuffs, we recommend that you use ribbing which has to be cut across the grain so that most of the stretch goes lengthwise.

Fold the fabric double with the right sides together. Place the pattern pieces on the fabric. Be sure to always follow the arrows on the pattern pieces, as it is very important that the greatest degree of stretch goes around the body and around the arms. Cut out the front, the back and the sleeves.

We recommend that you stabilize the fabric at the shoulder where you are going to place the snaps. Use lightweight press-on interfacing. Cut four small pieces the size of the shoulder facing. Press on the interfacing on the wrong side of the shoulder facing. Overcast the edges of the facing.

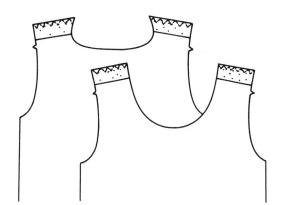

We also recommend stabilizing the ends of the neckband. Cut four pieces of press-on interfacing 1" x 1" (2.5 cm x 2.5 cm). Press on the interfacing on the wrong sides of the neckband.

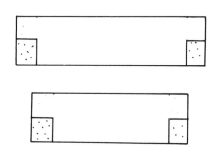

Fold the neckbands for the front and back lengthwise, right side to right side. Sew across the short ends. Turn the bands right side out.

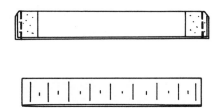

42

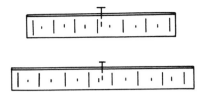

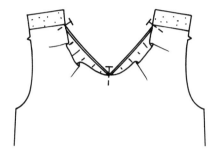

Divide each band in half and mark with a pin. Divide the front and the back neck openings in half with a pin. Pin the neckbands to the front and back neckline, right sides and raw edges together. Matching the pins, place the finished ends of the bands on the folding lines at the shoulders.

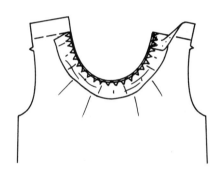

Fold the shoulder facing on the folding line over the bands to the right side. Sew the bands to the front and back opening, including the facing in the seam. Stretch the band while sewing to fit the openings. The easiest way to do this is to always have the smallest piece on top. In this case, the neck opening is underneath and the neckband on top. When sewing stretch fabric, you always stretch the smaller piece to fit the larger. This is the opposite method used for sewing non-stretch fabric, where you always ease the larger piece to the smaller. Turn the facing to the wrong side and press.

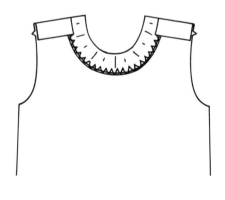

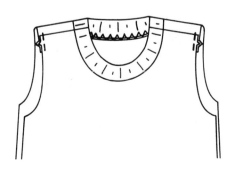

Overlap the front shoulder over the back shoulder, matching the notches. To keep the shoulders in place, sew a seam across close to the sleeve opening.

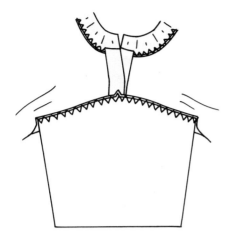

Sew in the sleeves by matching the notches at the shoulder and the underarm edges.

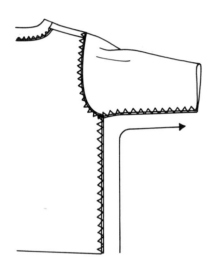

Sew the side seam and sleeve seam in one continuous operation, starting at the bottom of the shirt.

Sew the ends of the sleeve bands together, right side to right side, to form circles. Fold each band lengthwise, wrong sides together. Divide the bands and the sleeve openings in half with pins.

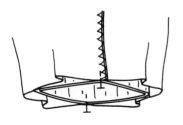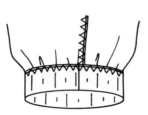

Pin the bands to the right side of the sleeve openings, matching the pins and the raw edges. Sew on the bands, stretching the bands to fit the openings.

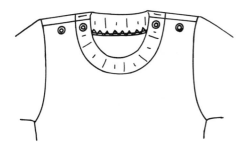

Attach two snaps at each shoulder. If you prefer, you may use buttons and buttonholes instead of snaps.

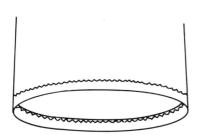

Hem the bottom edge of the T-shirt. First overcast the raw edges, and then turn the hem 1" (2.5 cm) to the wrong side and sew close to the overcasted edge. The best stitch to use is a narrow zigzag stitch.

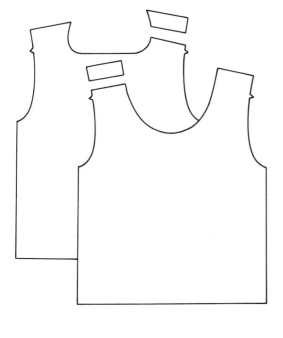

OPENING AT ONE SHOULDER
You may want to have only one shoulder that opens. In this case, eliminate the shoulder facing on one side by cutting the pattern on the folding line. Sew one shoulder seam using a ¼" (6 mm) seam allowance.

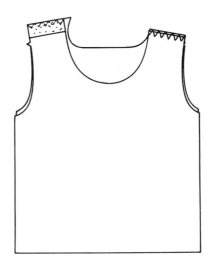

The neckband has to be cut in one piece, so use Master Pattern Pieces #4 and #5. Overlap the edges 1" (2.5 cm) and cut out the neckband. Stabilize the ends of the neckband and shoulder facing as previously described.

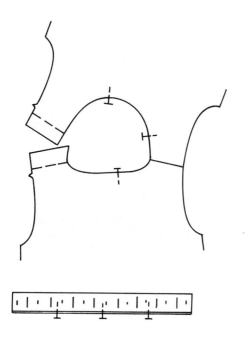

Finish off the ends of the neckband by folding the band double lengthwise and sew across the short ends. Turn the band to the right side. Divide the neckband and the neck opening into fourths with pins.

Start dividing at the folding line of the open shoulder. Pin the neckband to the neck opening with the right sides and the raw edges together, matching the pins and the ends of the neckband to the folding lines.

Fold the shoulder facing on the folding line over the bands to the right side. Sew on the neckband. Finish the T-shirt as previously described.

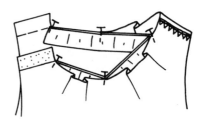

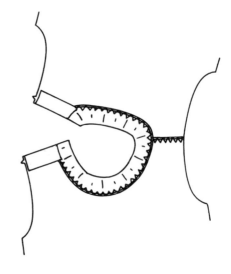

RIBBING NECKBAND WITH LACE

A pretty variation for baby girls' T-shirt can be made by adding lace to the neck opening. The lace will protrude below the neckband. Use a soft lace approximately 1" (2.5 cm) wide. Cut the lace twice the length of the neck opening from the folding line on one shoulder to the folding line on the other shoulder. Cut one piece for the front and one piece for the back, or if the opening is just on one shoulder, cut the lace in one piece. Fold a narrow hem on each end of the lace and hem.

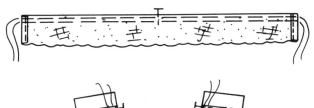

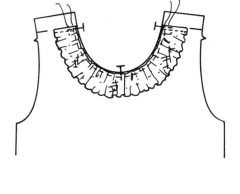

Gather the lace to fit the neck opening; baste the lace from folding line to folding line on the right side of the neck opening, raw edges together. Sew on the neckband as previously described. Remove the gathering stitches and the basting stitches. With the seam allowance toward the garment, stitch through lace and seam allowance close to the seam.

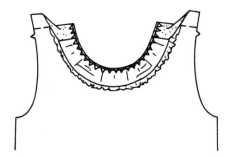

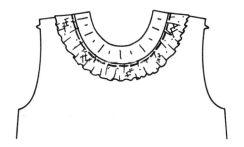

You can use the same procedures for attaching lace to the bottom of the sleeves, if you are using cuffs.

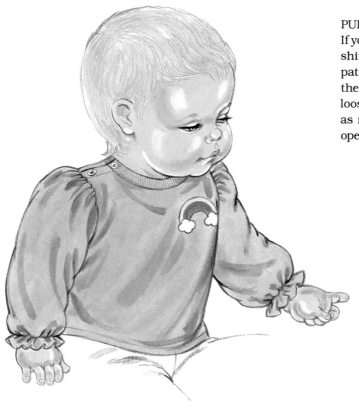

PUFF SLEEVES

If you are sewing a T-shirt for a little girl, a very attractive shirt may be made by using puff sleeves. Use Master pattern piece 27 for the sleeves. Sew a gathering stitch on the sleeve cap from mark to mark. Use long stitches with a loose thread tension. Pull the bobbin thread and gather as much as needed so that the sleeve will fit the sleeve opening. Sew on the sleeve as previously described.

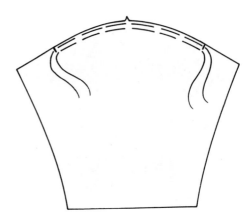

Hem the bottom of the sleeve with a narrow hem. Cut two strips of ⅛" (3 mm) wide elastic 5" (12.5 cm) long. Place the elastic 1" (2.5 cm) up from the bottom edge. Sew on the elastic, stretching the elastic to fit across the sleeve.

Finish T-shirt as previously described.

Instead of elastic, you can finish the bottom edge of the sleeve with a cuff. Shorten the length of the sleeve 2" (5 cm). Use Master Pattern piece #6 for the cuff. Sew on the cuff as previously described.

RUGBY SHIRT

A rugby shirt is a very practical garment for a baby. It is easy to pull over the baby's head. In addition, a rugby shirt gives you an excellent opportunity to use your imagination. By the use of contrasting colors, you can create a very attractive outfit. For instance, you can match the color of the collar and facing with the pants. The shirt has to be made using knit fabric, but you can use woven fabric for the collar and facing. The shirt can be made with either short or long sleeves.

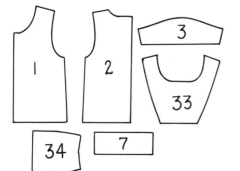

Use Master patterns:
- 1 - Front
- 2 - Back
- 3 - Sleeve
- 33 - Front Facing
- 34 - Collar
- 7 - Sleeveband, Short Sleeve

Eliminate the shoulder facing on both front and back. Cut away the facings on the folding lines.

Interface the facing and the collar with a fusible lightweight interfacing. Cut the interfacing for the entire facing. For the collar, cut the interfacing from the neckline edge to ½" (1.3 cm) past the folding line. Fuse to the wrong side.

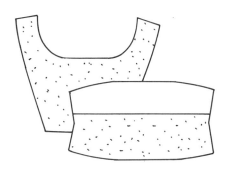

CENTER FRONT

Transfer the marking for the slit to the interfaced side of the facing and to the right front.

Pin the facing to the front, right sides together, matching the lines for the slit. Sew ⅛" (3 mm) on each side of the marked line; sew to a point at the dot. See illustration.

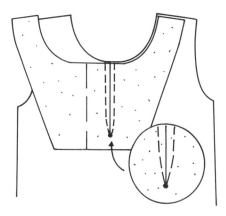

Cut an opening in between the sewing lines, following the line marked on the pattern. See illustration.

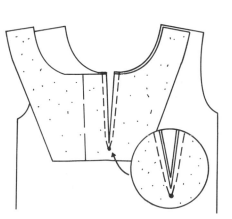

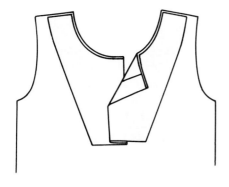

Fold the facing to the wrong side. On the right front, fold the facing on the folding line to form the tab. On the left front, fold the facing on the seam line and press.

Sew the front to the back at the shoulder seams.

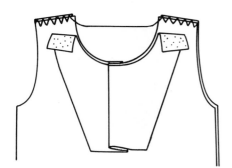

Fold the collar in half lengthwise, right sides together, and sew the ends. Turn the collar right side out and press.

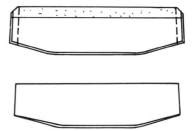

Pin the collar to the right side of the neck opening, matching the center back, dots on the collar to the shoulder seams, and the ends of the collar to the center front. On the right front, the center front is in the middle of the tab; on the left front, the center front is ⅜" (1 cm) from seam on the shirt. See illustration.

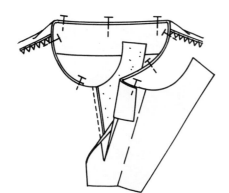

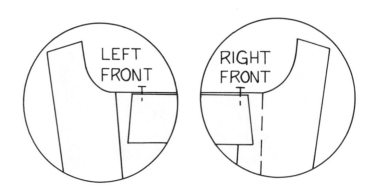

On the right front, fold the facing on the folding line to the right side over the collar and pin in place. On the left front, fold the facing on the seam line to the right side over the collar and pin in place. Sew the collar to the neck opening through all layers.

Overcast the raw edges together at the back neck opening. Turn the facing to the inside and press. Attach the ends of the facings to the shoulder seams.

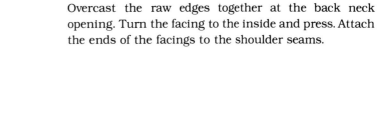

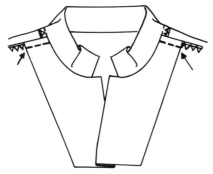

Overlap the left front over the right front and pin in place through all the layers. At the bottom of the slit, sew a ¼" x ¾" (6 mm x 2 cm) rectangle across the facing through all layers.

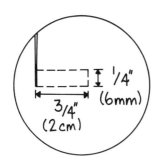

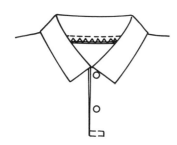

Finish the shirt by following the same procedures as used for the T-shirt. Apply two snaps to the front opening, or buttonholes and buttons may be used.

ROMPERS

A romper is a very practical one-piece garment and is ideal for summer or for warmer climates.

The top part of the romper is constructed the same way as the T-shirt. It looks very attractive if you use a contrasting color for the bands around the neck, arm and leg openings. This is a garment where you can really let your imagination go regarding appliques. (See Section 8.)

For a romper, we recommend using single knit, stretch velour, stretch terry or interlock.

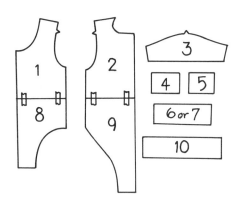

Use Master patterns:

 1 - Front
 2 - Back
 8 - Front Overlay
 9 - Back Overlay
 3 - Sleeve
 4 - Front Neckband
 5 - Back Neckband
 10 - Leg Band
 6 - Long Sleeve Cuff, or
 7 - Short Sleeveband

Start by overlapping pattern piece 8 on top of pattern piece 1. The top of pattern piece 8 should be placed on the line for overlay. Place pattern piece 9 on top of pattern piece 2 in the same manner.

Place the fabric right side to right side, and cut out the romper. Finish the top part of the romper the same way as the T-shirt.

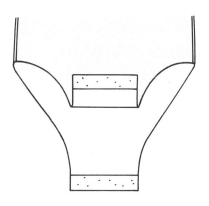

Cut two strips of lightweight press-on interfacing the length of the crotch and the width of the facing. Press on the interfacing, and overcast the raw edges on the bottom of the crotch.

Press on interfacing on the ends of the leg bands. Fold the bands for the leg openings, lengthwise, right side to right side, and sew across the short ends. Turn the band right side out.

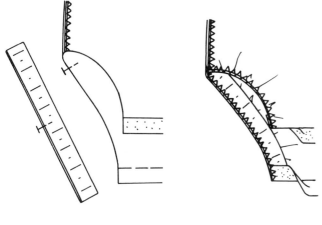

Divide each band in half and mark with a pin. Divide each leg opening in half and mark with a pin.

Pin the bands to the leg openings, right side and raw edges together, matching the pins with the finished ends of the bands on the folding lines at the crotch. Fold the crotch facing over the bands to the right side on the folding lines. Sew the bands to the leg openings, including the facing in the seam. While sewing, stretch the bands to fit the openings.

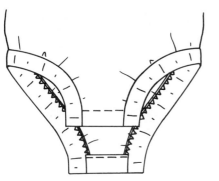

Turn the facing to the wrong side. Topstitch the facing to keep it in place. Attach four snaps to the crotch opening, match four female snaps on the front crotch opening and four male snaps on the back. The front crotch overlaps the back.

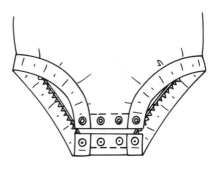

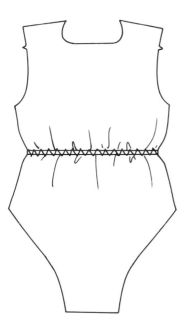

For a little more fitted romper, you can sew on a soft piece of elastic on the back at the waistline. When you cut out the romper, cut a piece of elastic 2½" (6 cm) shorter than the width of the back. Sew on the elastic from the side seam to the other side seam, stretching the elastic to fit the back.

ROMPER WITH WAISTBAND

A romper with a waistband looks like a two-piece outfit—a T-shirt with a waistband and panties—but it is actually one garment sewn together at the waist. It is easy to construct and can be very attractive by using appliques, contrasting fabrics and ribbings.

Piece the bottom and top pattern pieces together as for a regular romper. This pattern now has to be cut apart at the waist. From the bottom of the armholes on the front and the back, measure the distance from the armholes to the waist and mark. Draw a line across the pattern pieces. Use the following chart to give you the distance between the arm opening and the waist.

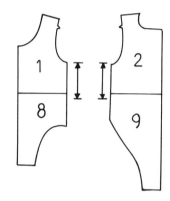

Small
3" (7.5 cm)

Medium
3½" (9 cm)

Large
4" (10 cm)

Extra Large
4½" (11.5 cm)

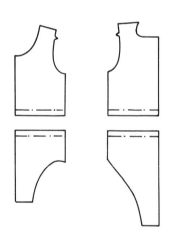

Cut the pattern pieces apart on this line. When you are cutting out the fabric, add ¼" (6 mm) for the seam allowance at the bottom and the top of the waist.

Use ribbing for the waistband Master pattern piece 15.

Sew the top part of the romper as described for a T-shirt. Sew the ends of the waistband together to form a circle. Fold the waistband double, wrong side to wrong side. Divide the bottom of the top and the waistband into fourths with pins.

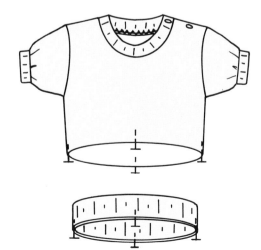

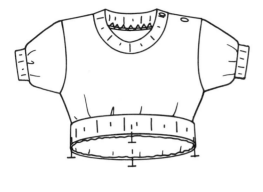

Pin on the waistband, right sides and raw edges together, matching the pins. Place the seam of the waistband at one side seam.

Sew the side seams of the panties. Finish the crotch and the leg openings as previously described.

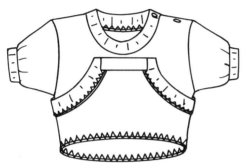

Pin the panties to the top over the waistband, right sides together, matching the center front, center back, and the side seams. Sew through all three layers, stretching the waistband to fit around the waist.

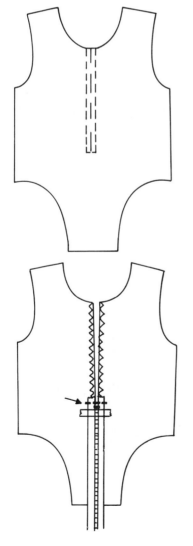

ROMPER WITH FRONT ZIPPER

You may wish to have an exposed zipper on the front and eliminate the shoulder snaps. This can easily be done. Use the same pattern pieces as used for a basic romper. On the front and back pattern pieces, cut away the facing on the shoulders on the folding lines.

You can have either a neckband or a collar when you use a zipper. Use Master pattern piece 34 for the collar or Master pattern piece 14 for the neckband. Cut out the romper as previously described.

Start out by inserting an exposed zipper at the center front. If you are working with very stretchy fabric, you should staystitch with a straight stitch close to where the opening will be. This will keep the fabric from stretching when you insert the zipper.

Cut a slit at the center front as long as the zipper. Overcast the raw edges.

Place the bottom edge of the zipper at the bottom of the slit. Be sure to place the right side of the zipper to the right side of the fabric. The bottom of the zipper teeth should be ¼" (6 mm) from the end of the opening. The zipper is now lying in the opposite direction from the cut opening. Hold the zipper in place with transparent tape.

Sew a few stitches, the width of the zipper teeth at the bottom of the slit to secure the zipper. Remove the tape. Flip the zipper into the correct position.

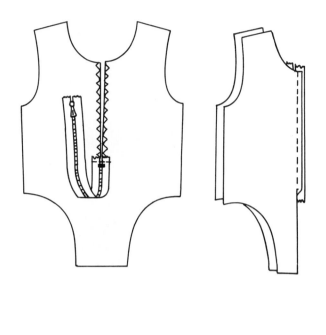

Fold one side of the fabric over the zipper, right side to right side, and sew as close as possible to the zipper teeth. The seam allowance will be very narrow. Follow the same procedure for the other side.

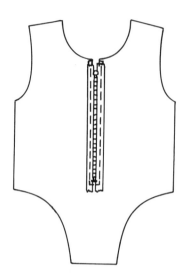

Sew the shoulder seams.

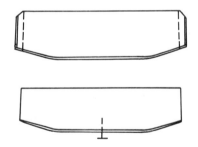

COLLAR

If you are using a collar, fold the collar on the folding line, right side to right side, and sew the ends of the collar. Turn the collar right side out.

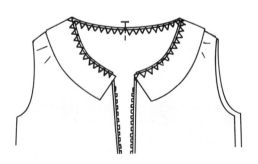

Mark the center back of the collar and the center back of the neck opening. Pin the collar, right side to right side, to the neck opening with the raw edges together, and matching the center back of the collar to the center back of the neck opening. Match the ends of the collar to the center front opening. Sew on the collar, using a ¼" (6 mm) seam allowance. Fold seam allowance toward garment, and sew close to the seam allowance through all layers.

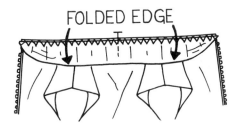

FOLDED EDGE

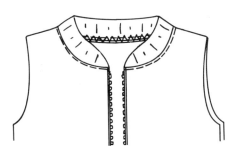

NECKBAND

If you decide to use a neckband instead of a collar when you are using a front zipper, cut out the neckband.

Fold the band lengthwise, wrong sides together. Divide the neckband in half with a pin. Mark the center back of the neck opening.

Pin the band to the right side of the neck opening, raw edges together, matching the center back and ends of neckband to the center front. Sew on the neckband, stretching band to fit neck opening. Fold seam allowance toward garment, and sew close to the seam through all layers.

Sew on the sleeves, matching the notch on the sleeve to the shoulder seam. Sew the side seam and sleeve seam in one continuous operation, starting at the bottom of the romper. Finish the sleeves and the leg openings in the same manner as previously described.

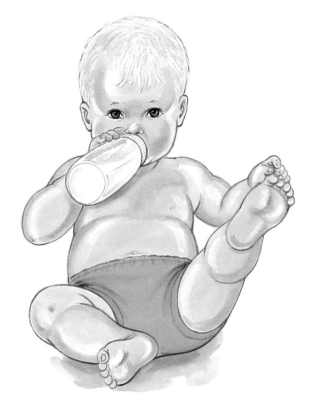

PANTIES

Panties can be made using regular white stretch fabric or you can use colorful prints to be worn over the diapers on a warm day. We suggest either a one- or two-way stretch fabric, single knit, interlock, or stretch terry. Remember that the greatest degree of stretch goes around the body.

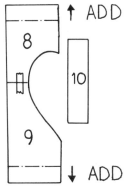

Use Master pattern pieces 8 and 9. Use pattern 10 for leg bands, and cut from ribbing.

Tape the crotch together by matching center lines at crotch eliminating the facing so that you end up with one pattern piece. To get the correct length for the panties, add to the front and back waistline. Use the following chart:

Small	Medium
3" (7.5 cm)	2½" (6.5 cm)
Large	Extra Large
2" (5 cm)	1½" (4 cm)

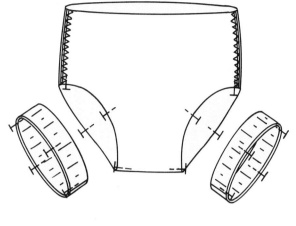

Place the back and the front of the panties together, right side to right side, and sew the side seams.

Sew the leg bands together, right side to right side, to form circles. Fold and press each band lengthwise, wrong sides together.

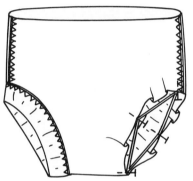

Divide the bands and the leg openings into fourths with pins. Pin the bands to the right side of the leg openings, raw edges together, matching the pins. Sew on the bands, stretching the bands to fit the openings.

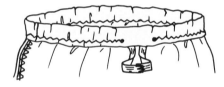

Overcast the opening at the waist, and turn ⅝" (1.5 cm) to the wrong side to form the casing. Use a ⅜" (1 cm) wide soft elastic. Cut one piece of elastic slightly smaller than the child's waist measurement, making sure that the elastic is not too tight around the child's waist.

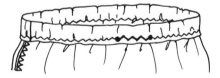

If you are making the panties for a gift or if the baby is not yet born, use this chart for the elastic measurement:

Small	Medium
17" (43 cm)	17½" (44 cm)
Large	Extra Large
18" (46 cm)	18½" (47 cm)

Sew the casing leaving a 1" (2.5 cm) opening for inserting the elastic. Insert the elastic through the opening, and sew the ends together. Close the opening.

PANTIES WITH LACE

As a little girl's panties very often show under the dress, they should be very pretty. One way to accomplish this is to attach lace to the back of the panties. Use lace approximately ½" (1.3 cm) wide. Cut as many strips as you wish to have. Gather the lace slightly by sewing a gathering stitch on one edge of the lace and then pull the bobbin thread.

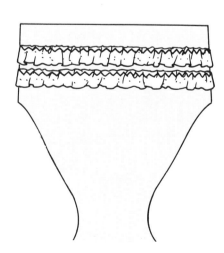

Sew on the lace **before** you sew the side seams using either a straight stitch or a narrow zigzag stitch. You can either overlap the lace slightly, or separate the strips. Finish sewing the panties as previously described.

Jogging Suit
Sweatshirts
Cardigan
Pants
Short Pants

SECTION **5** We all know that a baby is too small to do any jogging, however, this is the name used for a combination top and pants using sweatshirt fabric. This garment can be made using a wide variety of fabrics such as stretch velour, sweatshirt fleece, sweater fabric, double knit, etc. The construction is the same for all the different types of fabrics, however, if you are using sweater fabric, refer to Section 1 for the special instructions concerning this type of fabric.

The beginning of this Section will explain how to construct the top of the jogging suit and the various variations that may be used. Later on we will discuss the construction of the pants.

For the sweatshirt, use Master patterns:

    11 - Front
    12 - Back
    13 - Sleeve
    14 - Neckband
    15 - Waistband
    6 - Cuff

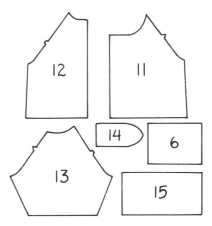

Place the fabric, right side to right side, and cut out the pattern pieces. We recommend using ribbing for the neckband, waistband and cuffs. When cutting out a raglan sleeve, we suggest that you mark the front and back raglan seams, as they are not identical and it is easy to sew them incorrectly. Place a piece of transparent tape on the wrong side and mark with a pencil on the tape on the front and back raglan seams.

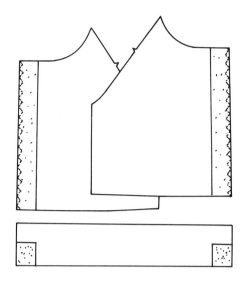

We recommend that you stabilize the front facing and the ends of the waistband with a press-on interfacing, as this type of fabric is soft and stretchy. We also recommend that you overcast the front raw edges.

Sew the back and front raglan seams, matching the notches.

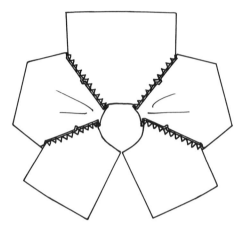

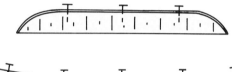

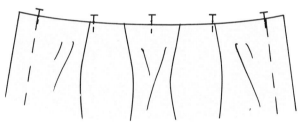

Now fold the neckband lengthwise, wrong sides together, and press. Divide the neckband and neck opening into fourths with pins. Mark the center back. Place a pin halfway between the center back and the folding line on the fronts.

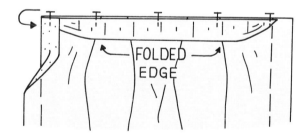

FOLDED EDGE

Pin the neckband to the neck opening, right side to right side, with the raw edges together. Match the pins and place the ends of the band to the folding lines on the front.

Fold the front facing on the folding line to the right side over the neckband. Sew the band to the neck opening, including the facing in the seam. Stretch the band to fit the neck opening. Turn the facing to the wrong side and press the facing on the folding line.

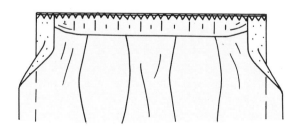

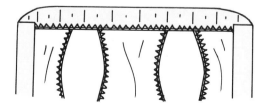

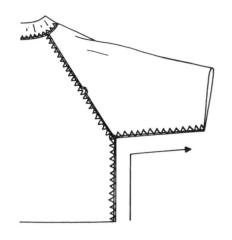

Sew the side seams and the sleeve seams in one operation, starting at the bottom of the jacket, matching the underarm seams.

Fold the waistband lengthwise, right sides together. Sew across the short ends.

Turn right side out. Divide the waistband and the bottom of the jacket into fourths with pins. The first pin should be at the folding line.

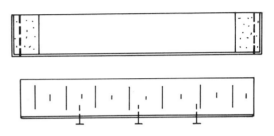

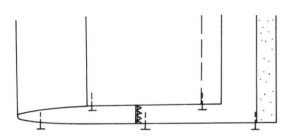

Pin the waistband to the bottom edge of the jacket, right side to right side, matching the pins. The ends of the waistband should be at the folding lines. Fold the facing to the right side over the waistband, sew on the waistband including the facing in the seam.

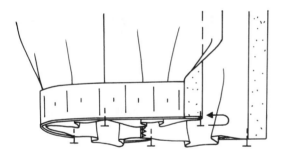

Turn the facing to the wrong side. Sew the facing close to the overcasted edges. This step can be eliminated but as baby clothes are washed very often, unless you sew down the facing, it will tend to roll up after washing.

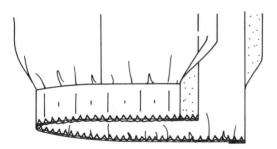

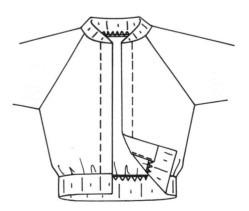

Sew on the cuffs on the bottom of the sleeves; use the same method as described for the T-shirts in Section 4, page 44.

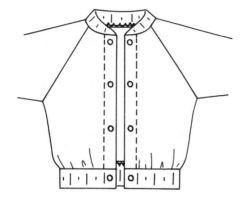

Place one snap ⅜" (1 cm) down from the neckline seam, one at the middle of the waistband, and add two more snaps an equal distance apart. Make sure that you apply the snaps at the correct position, as it is almost impossible to change them. Remember that girl's clothing closes from the right, and boy's from the left.

Instead of snaps, you may wish to use buttons and buttonholes.

HOOD

Instead of using a neckband, you may want to use a hood to help keep the baby warm. Eliminate the neckband and use Master Pattern piece 19 for the hood. Place the fabric, right side to right side, put the top part of the hood on the fold. Cut out the hood.

Press the facing to the wrong side on the folding line; sew down the facing close to the raw edges. Place the hood, double, right side to right side, and sew the back seam.

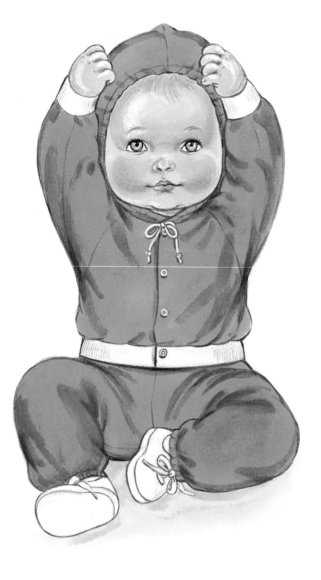

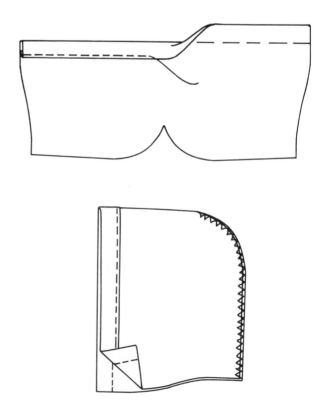

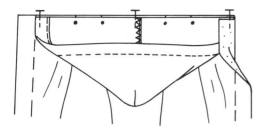

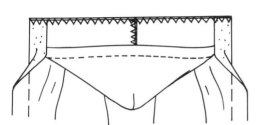

Sew the front and the back raglan seams. Pin the hood to the neck opening, right side to right side, matching the center backs. Match the dots on the hood with the front and back raglan seams, and the edges of the hood to the folding line on the fronts. Fold the front facing to the right side on the folding line over the hood. Sew on the hood and include the facing in the same seam. Turn the facing to the wrong side. Finish the jacket as previously described.

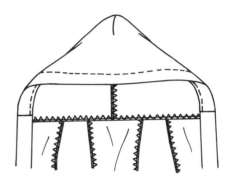

SWEATSHIRT WITH LACE AND RIBBON

You can make a very pretty sweatshirt for a baby girl by adding lace and ribbon to the front and hood.

Cut two pieces of ribbon and pregathered lace or eyelet the length of the front. Pin the lace to the wrong side of ribbon with the lace extending and baste close to edge of ribbon. If gathered edge of lace is finished with binding, remove the binding to reduce bulk.

Pin the lace and ribbon to front with right sides up and edge without the lace 1" (2.5 cm) from the folding line on front. Sew close to both edges of the ribbon.

Follow the same procedures to apply the lace and ribbon to the hood. Sew the sweatshirt following the same instructions as for a regular sweatshirt.

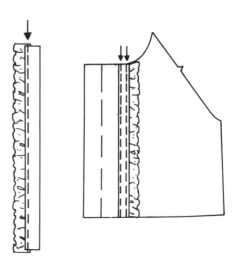

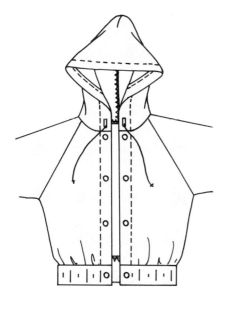

HOOD WITH DRAWSTRING

If you plan to use a drawstring in the hood, you need buttonholes for the drawstring. These are placed where the drawstring will come through the hood.

Mark a ½" (1.3 cm) buttonhole 1½" (4 cm) from the front edge and ⅝" (1.5 cm) up from the neckline on each front edge of the hood. To stabilize the fabric under the buttonhole, place a piece of interfacing on the wrong side and make the buttonhole through the fabric and the interfacing. The buttonhole should be made BEFORE you start constructing the hood.

After you have sewn on the hood, insert the drawstring in the casing from one buttonhole to the other buttonhole.

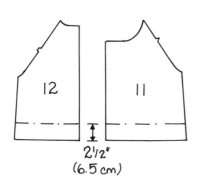

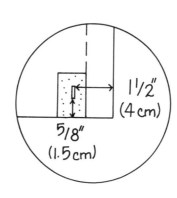 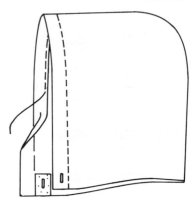

DRAWSTRING AT BOTTOM EDGE

As a variation, you may want to use a drawstring at the bottom of the jacket instead of using a waistband. Lengthen the back and front pattern pieces 2½" (6.5 cm) before you cut out the fabric.

The jacket is constructed in the same way up to the point where you are attaching the waistband. Mark the position for the buttonholes on the bottom edge of each front 1⅝" (4.2 cm) from the front edge and ¾" (2 cm) up from the bottom edge. Place a piece of interfacing under the position of the buttonholes. Make the buttonholes.

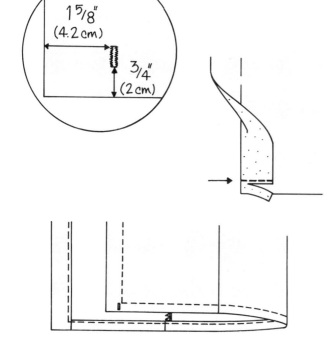

At the bottom edge of the jacket, fold the facing on the folding line to the right side and sew ⅝" (1.5 cm) from the bottom edge. Trim the seam allowance on the facing. Turn the facing to the inside and press.

Fold the bottom hem ⅝" (1.5 cm) to the wrong side to form the casing. Now sew the front facings and the casing in one operation. Insert the drawstring through the buttonholes on the bottom edge.

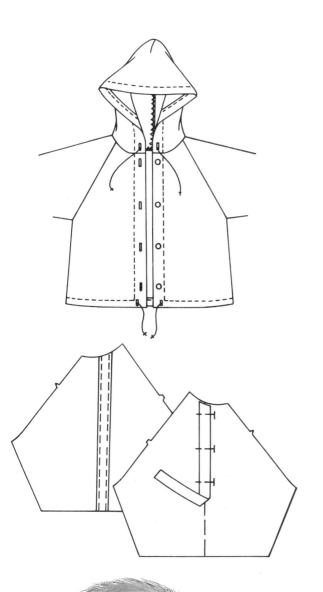

Mark the position of the buttonholes: Top buttonhole ⅜" (1 cm) down from the neck opening seam, bottom buttonhole ¾" (2 cm) up from the bottom edge, and add two more an equal distance apart. Make the buttonholes; sew on buttons to match.

TRIM

A little jogging suit can be made to look very attractive with the use of trim running down the length of the arms and the legs. When you have cut out the sleeves, cut two lengths of trim the length of the sleeves. Pin the trim to the middle of the sleeves with the right side up. Sew the trim to the sleeves, sewing on each edge of the trim. Do not cut out the fabric underneath the trim.

The use of trim will enable you to use your imagination. It can be horizontal across the jacket, across the sleeves, or both. How to attach the trim to the legs will be explained later in this Section.

PULL-ON SHIRT WITH SIDE CLOSURE

Instead of having a center front opening, you may want to have an opening at the left front raglan seam.

Use Master patterns:
- 11 - Front
- 12 - Back
- 13 - Sleeve
- 6 - Cuff
- 15 - Waistband (optional)

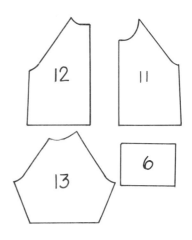

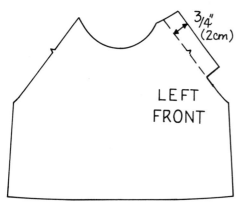

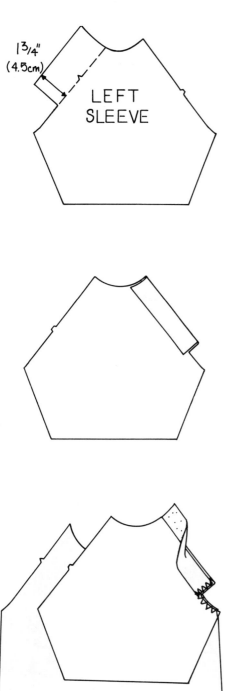

Trace pattern piece 11. Make a complete front, using a center front line. The pattern pieces for the left sleeve and the front have to be altered so that you will have a facing for the opening on the left side. Change the pattern pieces as illustrated.

If you do not plan to use a waistband, remember to lengthen the front and the back 2½" (6.5 cm).

For the neckband, cut a piece of ribbing, across the grain 10" (25.5 cm) long and 2¼" (5.5 cm) wide.

Cut out the shirt. Cut two pieces of press-on interfacing 1" (2.5 cm) wide and the length of the facing. Press on the interfacing. Overcast the edge of the facing.

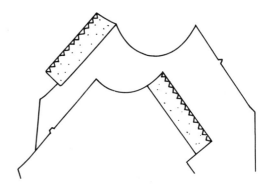

On the left sleeve, press the facing to the wrong side 1" (2.5 cm) from the edge and pin. Place the sleeve and the front, right side to right side. Sew the left front raglan seam from the underarm to ¼" (6 mm) past the raw edges of the facing; lower the needle, turn the fabric, and sew the width of the facing.

Press in place.

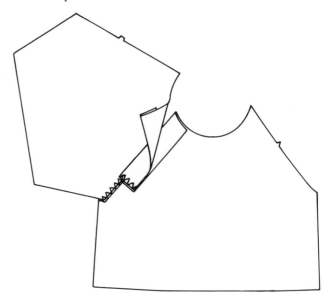

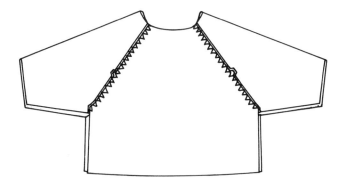

Sew the other front raglan seam and the back raglan seams.

Stabilize the ends of the neckband with press-on interfacing. Fold the neckband double lengthwise, right sides together. Sew across both short ends. Turn the band to the right side. Divide the neckband into fourths with pins.

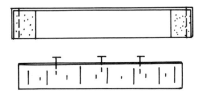

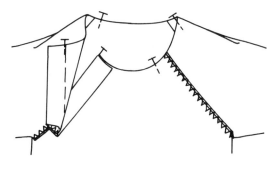

Divide the neck opening into fourths between folding lines and mark with pins. Pin the band to the right side of the neck opening, raw edges together, matching the pins and placing the finished edges of the bands on the folding lines. Fold the facings over the band to the right side.

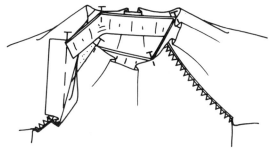

Sew the band to the neck opening, including the facing in the seam. Stretch the band to fit the neck opening. Turn the facing to the wrong side.

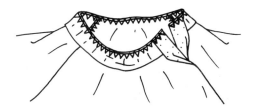

Sew the side seams and the sleeve seams in one operation, starting at the bottom of the shirt.

Apply snaps to the left shoulder opening. If you prefer, you can use buttons and buttonholes.

Attach the cuffs to the sleeves and apply waistband using the same procedure as previously described. If not using waistband, hem the bottom edge.

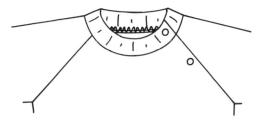

SWEATSHIRT WITH SLIT OPENING

This shirt is easy to pull over the baby's head as the front opening is long enough and therefore you do not need an opening at the raglan seam. Use sweatshirt fabric for the shirt, lightweight woven fabric for the tab facing and ribbing for the neckband, waistband and cuffs.

Use Master patterns:
- 11 - Front
- 12 - Back
- 13 - Sleeve
- 18 - Front Tab Facing
- 14 - Neckband
- 6 - Cuffs
- 15 - Waistband

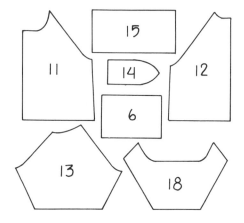

Cut pattern piece 11 on the center front, be sure to cut the front and the back on the fold. Cut out the sleeves. Cut out the pattern piece for the front tab facing. Be sure to place the pattern piece with the printed side of the pattern up on the right side of the fabric. Using lightweight press-on interfacing, press the interfacing to the wrong side of the tab facing. Transfer the slit line to the interfaced side of the facing. On the front, mark a center front line from the top to the bottom. On the right front, mark a line for the slit ½" (1.3 cm) from the center front line and the length of the slit on the tab facing.

Pin the tab facing to the front, right sides together, matching the lines for the slit. Sew ⅛" (3 mm) down one side of the slit and up the other side. Cut the slit open.

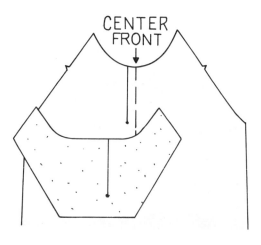

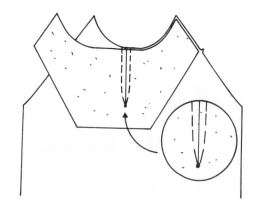

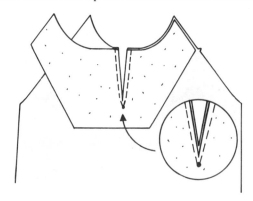

68

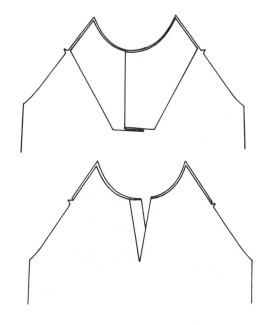

On the right front, fold the facing on the folding line and press to form the tab. On the left front, fold the entire facing to the wrong side and press.

Sew the front and back raglan seams.

Fold the neckband double lengthwise, wrong sides together. Divide the neckband in half; mark with a pin. Mark the center back of the neck opening.

Pin the neckband to the neck opening, right sides and raw edges together, matching the center back and pin on the neckband. On the right front, place the end of the neckband on the folding line on the tab. On the left front, place the end of the neckband on the seam for the facing. Sew the neckband to the neck opening.

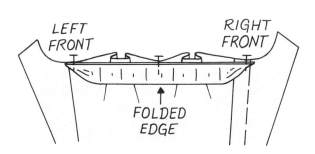

LEFT FRONT RIGHT FRONT

FOLDED EDGE

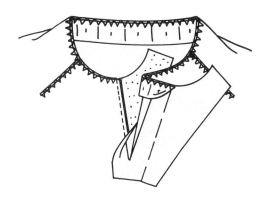

Fold the front facings to the right side over the neckband. On the right front, fold the facing on the folding line. On the left front, fold the facing on the seam line. Sew the facing to the neck opening on top of the seam used for sewing on the neckband. Fold the facing to the inside and attach the ends of the facing to the front raglan seams.

Overlap the left front over the right front and pin through all layers. At the bottom of the slit, sew a ¼" (6 mm) rectangle across the facing through all layers.

Apply two snaps to the front opening or you can use buttons and buttonholes. Sew side and sleeve seams. Apply cuffs and waistband following the procedures for cuffs on page 44.

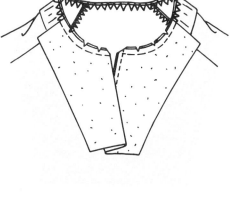

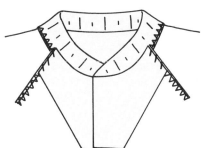

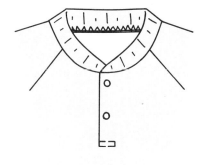

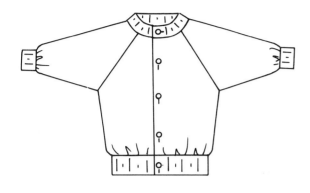

CARDIGAN SWEATER

You can make a very attractive garment for a baby when you use sweater fabric. See Section 1 for information on sweater fabrics.

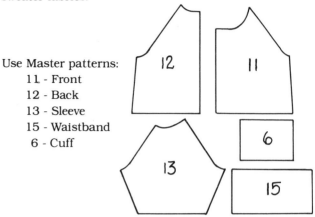

Use Master patterns:
- 11 - Front
- 12 - Back
- 13 - Sleeve
- 15 - Waistband
- 6 - Cuff

For the neckband, cut a piece of ribbing across the grain 11" (28 cm) long and 2¼" (5.5 cm) wide.

Sew the front and back raglan seams as described previously.

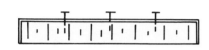

Fold the neckband double, lengthwise, wrong sides and raw edges together.

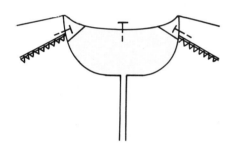

Divide the neckband and neck opening into fourths with pins.

Pin the neckband to the neck opening with right sides and raw edges together, matching pins and ends of the neckband to the edges of front. Sew on the neckband, stretching it to fit the neck opening.

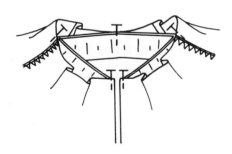

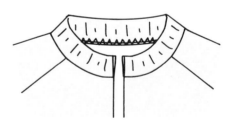

Sew the side seams, the sleeve seams and sew on the waistband as described previously.

As sweater fabric is a more loosely knitted fabric, the easiest method of finishing the front of a cardigan is with a strip of grosgrain ribbon. We recommend that you preshrink the ribbon before you use it. Cut two lengths of ⅝" (1.5 cm) wide grosgrain ribbon long enough for the front plus 1" (2.5 cm). Overlap the ribbon on the right side of each front to the folding line, ½" (1.3 cm) should extend on the top and the bottom. Sew on the ribbon close to the inner edge with a straight stitch.

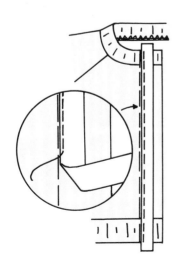

Cut away the facing underneath the ribbon.

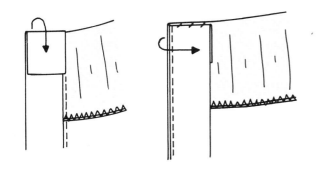

Turn the ribbon to the wrong side. The buttons and buttonholes will hold the ribbon in place. Fold under the bottom and the top ends of the ribbon and finish with a few hand stitches.

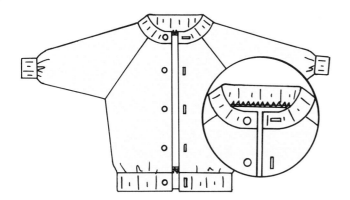

On a round neck cardigan, the buttonhole on the neckband is horizontal and the other buttonholes are vertical. The buttonholes should be placed in the middle of the grosgrain ribbon.

For a boy's cardigan, place the buttonholes on the left front; for a girl's, on the right front.

PANTS

Use the same fabric for the pants as you used for the jacket if you want to have a matching jogging suit. If only constructing pants, you can use almost any type of fabric, stretch or non-stretch. Use Master pattern 16. Cut out two pieces for the pants.

Fold each piece, right side to right side, and sew the inside leg seams. Place one leg inside the other leg, right sides together, matching the inside leg seams. Sew the center front and the center back seam. Sew from the front waist to the back waist.

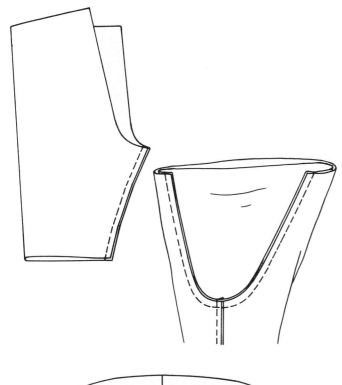

Overcast the top edge of the pants. Fold a ⅝" (1.5 cm) hem to the wrong side for the casing, and sew close to the raw edge. Leave a 1" (2.5 cm) opening so you can insert the elastic. Cut one length of elastic to fit the baby's waist. If you do not know the measurement, use the following chart. Be sure not to have the elastic too tight. Use ⅜" (1 cm) wide elastic.

APPROXIMATE MEASUREMENT CHART FOR WAIST ELASTIC:

Small	Medium
16" (40.5 cm)	16½" (42 cm)
Large	Extra Large
17" (43 cm)	17½" (44.5 cm)

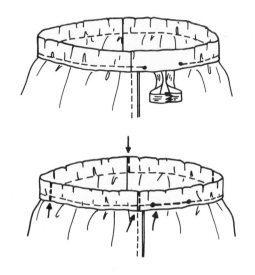

Insert the elastic through the casing. Sew the ends of the elastic together and close the opening. To keep the elastic from rolling in the casing, distribute gathers evenly, and from the right side, sew across the width of the elastic at the center front, center back and the sides.

Use Master Pattern piece #17 for the cuffs. Sew the ends of the cuffs, right sides together. Fold the cuffs double, wrong sides and raw edges together. Divide the cuffs and the bottom edge of the legs in half with pins.

Pin the cuffs to the bottom edge of the legs with the right sides and the raw edges together, matching the inside leg seams and the pins. Sew on the cuffs, stretching the cuffs to fit the leg openings.

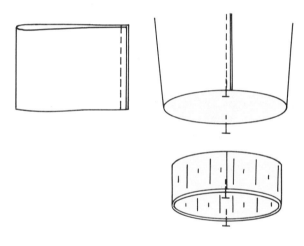

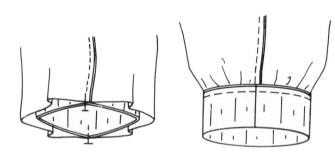

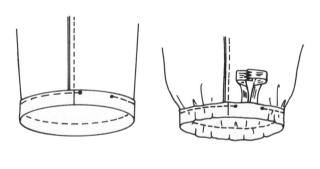

PANTS WITHOUT CUFFS

The pants can be made without cuffs. Add 2" (5 cm) to the length of the pants when you are cutting out the fabric. Hem the bottom edge.

If you plan to use elastic at the bottom of the legs, make a casing by folding ⅝" (1.5 cm) to the wrong side and sew, leaving an opening to insert the elastic. Cut two pieces of ⅜" (1 cm) wide elastic 8" (20 cm) long.

Insert the elastic into the casing and sew the ends together. Finish sewing the casing seams.

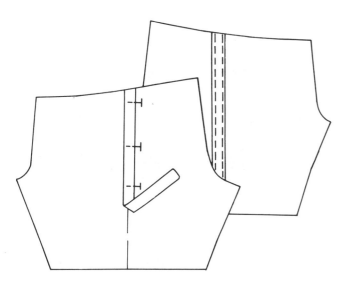

TRIM

Jogging suit pants can be made to look very attractive with the use of trim. Pin the trim to the legs before you sew the pants together. Cut two strips of trim the length of the legs.

Pin the trim to the middle of each leg. Sew the trim to the legs, close to the edges of the trim. Do not cut out the fabric underneath the trim.

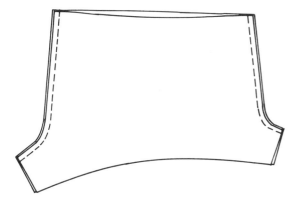

SHORT PANTS

Short pants can be worn by either boys or girls. The pattern is the same; the color of the fabric will determine if they are to be worn by a boy or a girl.

A pair of girl's panties can be very attractive, especially if they are constructed using the same fabric as the dress.

You can use lightweight non-stretch fabric or stretch fabric. Use Master pattern 16; cut the pattern on the cutting line for short pants.

Sew the center back and center front seams.

Sew the inside leg seams.

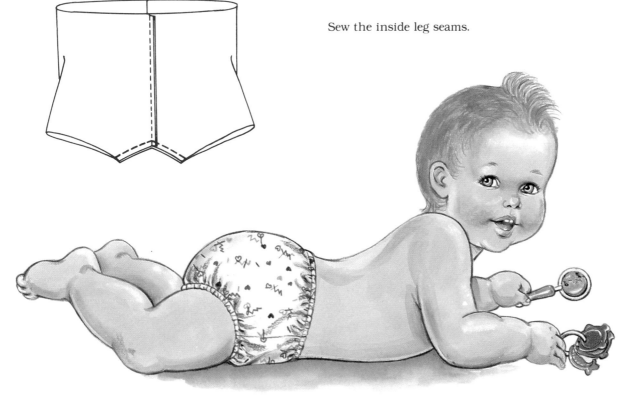

ELASTIC MEASUREMENT CHART FOR LEGS:

Small	Medium
9½" (24 cm)	10" (25 cm)
Large	Extra Large
10⅜" (26 cm)	10¾" (27.5 cm)

ELASTIC MEASUREMENT CHART FOR WAIST:

Small	Medium
16" (40.5 cm)	16½" (42 cm)
Large	Extra Large
17" (43 cm)	17½" (44.5 cm)

Overcast the raw edges around the waist and the leg openings. Turn ⅝" (1.5 cm) for the casing to the wrong side around the waist and the leg openings. Sew the casing seams close to the overcasted edges, leaving 1" (2.5 cm) opening to be used to insert the elastic. Cut two pieces of ¼" (6 mm) wide elastic for the legs and one for the waist. Insert the elastic.

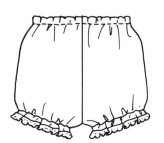

PANTIES WITH LACE

A little girl's panties can be made very attractive by adding lace to the bottom of the legs. It is easier to sew on the lace before you sew the panties together. Cut two strips of lace the width of the legs. Use approximately ⅝" (1.5 cm) wide lace. Pin the right side of the lace to the right side of the bottom edge of the legs. Sew on the lace using a ¼" (6 mm) seam allowance. Press the seam allowance toward the panties. On the right side, topstitch close to the seam through all layers.

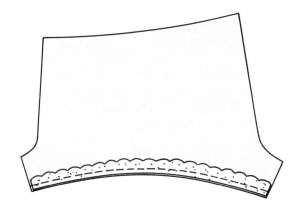

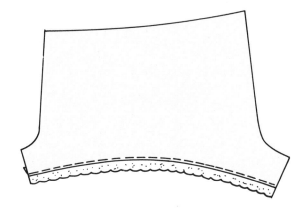

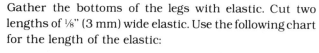

Gather the bottoms of the legs with elastic. Cut two lengths of ⅛" (3 mm) wide elastic. Use the following chart for the length of the elastic:

Small	Medium
7½" (19 cm)	8" (20.5 cm)
Large	Extra Large
8½" (21.5 cm)	9" (23 cm)

Sew on the elastic 1" (2.5 cm) up from the bottom of the legs. Sew over the elastic, stretching the elastic to fit the leg.

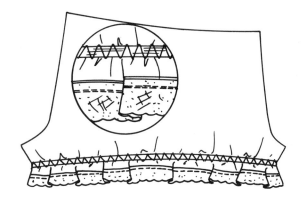

Finish sewing the panties as previously described.

Bib Overalls
Bib Pants
Bib Shorts

SECTION

6 After the baby is a few months old and starts crawling, overalls are very practical, and in addition, they can be constructed very easily and quickly.

Overalls are an excellent garment to which you can add appliques, numbers, letters or maybe you would like to have the baby's initials. When you are going to use appliques, etc., always do this BEFORE you have constructed the garment as it is easier to do this when the pieces of the garment are separate. However, as the overalls have a center front seam, this seam should be sewn before you put on the applique.

You can use stretch fabric or sturdy cotton fabric for everyday use.

Use Master patterns:

    16 - Pants
    31 - Overlay
    32 - Shoulder Straps
    17 - Cuffs (optional)

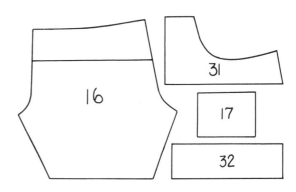

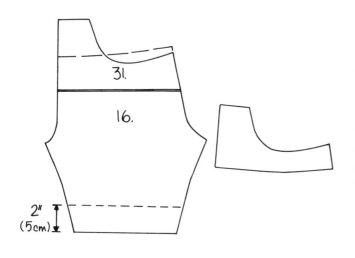

Trace the pattern size you need for both the pants and the overlay. Place the overlay on the marked line on the pants pattern, matching the center front and the center back. Cut two.

You will need a facing piece; trace the overlay following the line marked for facing and cut two. The overalls can be made with or without cuffs. Decide which style you want before you cut the fabric as you will have to add approximately 2" (5 cm) to the length if you do not use cuffs.

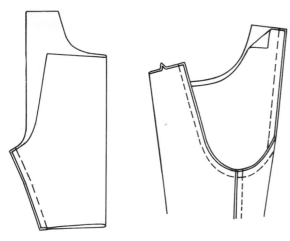

Sew the inside leg seams.

Place one leg inside the other leg, right sides together, matching the inside leg seams. Sew the center front and the center back seam from the back waist to the top of the bib. Sew the center front and the center back of the facing. Overcast the raw edges of the bottom of the facing.

Fold the shoulder straps double, lengthwise, right side to right side. Sew down one long side and one short side. Trim one corner and turn the straps right side out and press. Topstitch close to the edge around the entire strap.

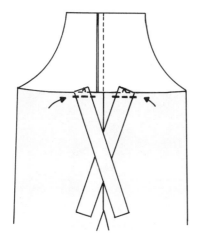

Place the strap on the right side of the back with the center of the strap at the notch. Sew close to the raw edges to hold the straps in place.

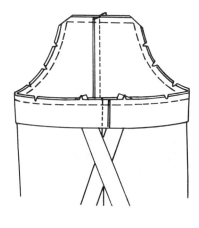

Place the facing, right side to right side, at the top of the pants. Sew around the facing. Cut the corners and clip the curved seam allowances. Turn the facing to the inside and press.

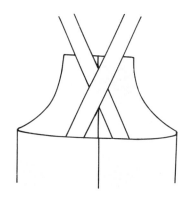

Mark the location for the ends of the elastic as indicated on the pattern piece. From this mark, topstitch all the way around to the other mark ⅜" (1 cm) from the edge. Cut one strip of ¼" (6 mm) wide elastic. Use the following chart:

Small	Medium
8" (20 cm)	9" (23 cm)
Large	Extra Large
10" (25.5 cm)	11" (28 cm)

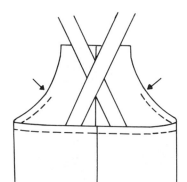

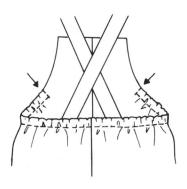

Insert the elastic through the opening underneath the facing using a safety pin. When you come close to the end of the elastic, sew across the end of the elastic through all thicknesses to keep the elastic in place. Pull the elastic to the other mark and secure the elastic.

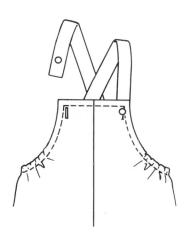

Topstitch the front of the bib ⅜" (1 cm) from the edge. Make two buttonholes at the top of the bib ½" (1.3 cm) from the top and the side edges. Sew a button on the strap.

If you plan to use cuffs, put them on in the same manner as described for pants in Section 5, page 72. If you are not using cuffs, hem the bottom edge.

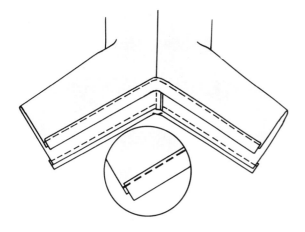

SNAPS ON INSIDE LEG SEAMS

You can use snaps on the inside leg seams and the crotch. This makes it much easier to change the baby's diapers. Before you cut out the overalls, add ⅜" (1 cm) to the inside leg seams.

We suggest that you use bias tape to finish the leg and crotch openings. Cut two lengths of ½" (1.3 cm) wide single fold bias tape the same length as the inside leg seam, measured from the bottom of one leg to the bottom of the other leg.

Overlap the tape ¼" (6 mm) on the right side of the leg opening. Sew a seam close to the edge of the tape.

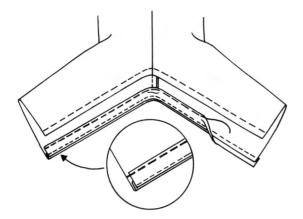

Fold the bias tape to the wrong side. Sew a second seam on the other edge of the tape.

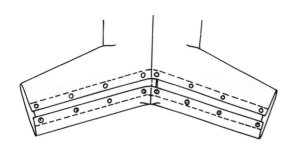

If you are not using cuffs, hem the legs. Apply the snaps to the inside leg, place the bottom snap at the top of the hem. The number of snaps will depend upon the length of the legs.

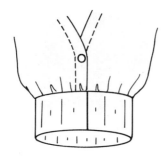

If you are using cuffs, apply the snaps, place the bottom snap 2" (5 cm) up from the bottom of the leg. Close the snaps and stitch across close to the edge. Sew on the cuff as previously described.

EYELET TRIM

A pretty variation can be made by adding eyelet or lace to the bib and the shoulder straps.

Sew the bib overalls as described previously to the point of sewing on the facing.

Measure the bib from mark for end of elastic on one side to mark on the other side and cut the eyelet twice that length.

Sew gathering stitches on the eyelet ¼" (6 mm) from edge and again in the middle of the seam allowance.

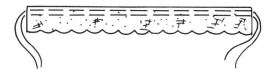

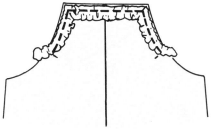

Pin the eyelet to the top edge of the bib, right sides together, with ends of eyelet at marks for end of elastic. Pull up gathering stitches to fit, adjusting gathers evenly. Fold ends of eyelet toward the raw edges as shown. Sew, using a ¼" (6 mm) seam allowance.

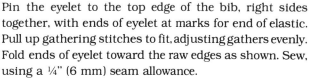

Cut two pieces of eyelet twice the length of the shoulder strap. Gather the eyelet and pin to one side of the shoulder strap. Fold under the end of the lace ⅜" (1 cm). Sew the lace to the shoulder strap. Repeat for other strap.

Fold shoulder strap, double lengthwise, right sides together and sew the long edge and the short side which has the eyelet folded under. Turn right side out.

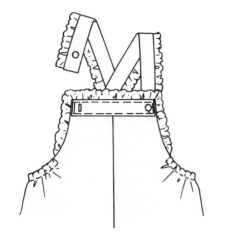

Finish the overalls as described previously.

If desired, add a piece of trim to the top edge of the bib. Place the trim along the top edge of the bib with right sides up; fold under the raw edges at the ends and sew close to each edge of trim. If desired, add the same eyelet to the bottom edge of the legs.

SHORT BIB OVERALLS

If you prefer short legs, which will give a very cute summer outfit especially if you use a lightweight cotton fabric, cut off the legs on the pattern piece on the line for short pants.

Sew the overalls as previously described.

Overcast the raw edges around the leg openings. Turn ⅝" (1.5 cm) for the casing to the wrong side around the leg openings. Sew the casing seams close to the overcasted edges, leaving 1" (2.5 cm) openings to be used to insert the elastic.

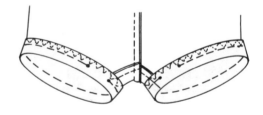

Cut two pieces of ¼" (6 mm) wide elastic for the legs using the following chart:

Small	Medium
9½" (24 cm)	10" (25 cm)
Large	Extra Large
10⅜" (26 cm)	10¾" (27.5 cm)

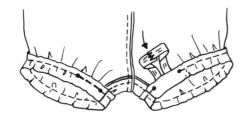

Insert the elastic into the casing and sew the ends together. Finish sewing the casing seams.

POCKETS

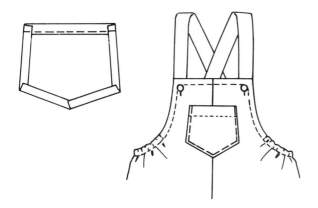

A pocket looks very attractive either at the front of the bib or on one of the legs. The size and shape of the pocket depends upon the size of the bib. This is where you have to use your own imagination.

When you have cut out the pocket, turn under the top edge ½" (1.3 cm) and topstitch across close to the edge. Fold under all raw edges ½" (1.3 cm) and press.

Sew on the pocket close to the folded edge where you wish it to be placed.

To be more creative, you can make pockets in various designs such as a little heart. When you have decided on the design, cut out the pocket in two thicknesses.

Place the pieces, right side to right side, and sew around the edges, leaving an opening large enough to turn the pocket right side out. Close the opening. Sew on the pocket by topstitching close to the edge.

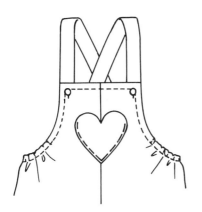

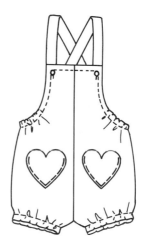

BIB PANTS

A regular pair of pants have a tendency to slide down over the baby's hips, but the shoulder straps on a pair of bib pants will prevent this.

Bib pants are a very practical outfit for a hot summer day. We recommend using a lightweight cotton fabric for bib pants with short legs. For a warmer garment, we suggest that you use the long legs version. Used with a T-shirt or blouse, it makes a complete outfit.

Bib pants can be used for either a boy or a girl depending upon the color, fabric, trim and appliques.

We will start by giving you the instructions for a plain pair of bib pants. Later on, we will explain how to make the pants very attractive with variations such as appliques, etc.

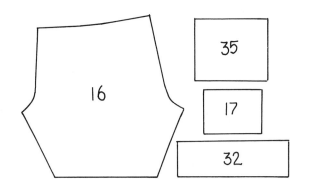

Use Master pattern pieces:

> 16 - Pants
> 35 - Bib
> 32 - Shoulder Straps
> 17 - Leg Cuff (optional)

Decide if you want short or long legs. If using long legs and you do not want the leg cuffs, add approximately 2" (5 cm) to the bottom of the legs. Cut out the pattern pieces.

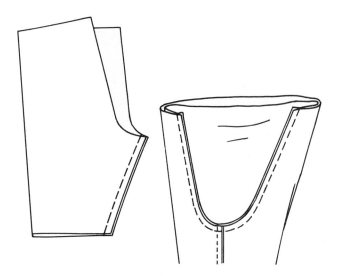

Sew the inside leg seams.

Place one leg inside the other leg, right sides together, matching the inside leg seams. Sew the center front and center back seams.

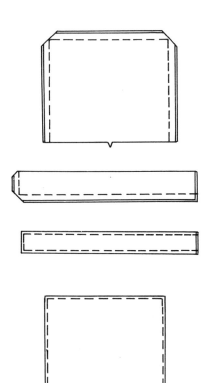

Place the two bib pieces, right side to right side, and sew around three sides, leaving the bottom edge open. Trim the corners and turn the bib right side out.

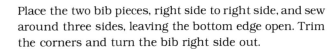

Fold the shoulder straps, right side to right side, lengthwise. Sew one long side and one short side on each strap. Turn the straps right side out.

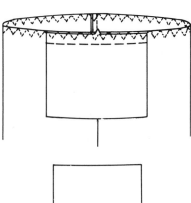

Topstitch around the three sides of the bib and the shoulder straps close to the edges.

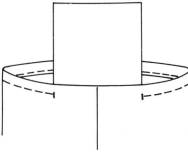

Sew on the bib by placing the bib, right side to right side, matching the center of the bib with the center front at the waist. Sew across the bib ⅝" (1.5 cm) down from the edge.

Overcast the raw edges around the waist. Fold ⅝" (1.5 cm) to the wrong side to form a casing. Sew close to the overcasted edge, starting at one edge of the bib, around the back to the other edge of the bib. You do NOT sew across the bib.

Cut one length of ⅜" (1 cm) wide elastic. Use the following chart for the length:

Small	Medium
10" (25 cm)	10½" (26.5 cm)
Large	Extra Large
11" (28 cm)	11½" (29 cm)

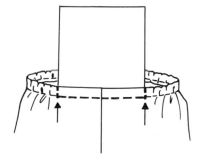

Using a safety pin, insert the elastic through the opening underneath the bib. Sew across the end of the elastic through all thicknesses, close to the edge of the bib. Pull the elastic to the other end of the bib and sew across the end of the elastic through all thicknesses. Sew across the bib using the same seam allowance as used for the casing.

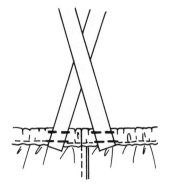

Place the unfinished ends of the straps, 1" (2.5 cm) in from the center back seam. See illustration. Sew a seam across the top and the bottom of the elastic to keep the straps in place.

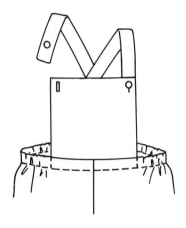

Make two buttonholes on the top part of the bib approximately ¼" (6 mm) down from the top and ½" (1.3 cm) in from the side of the bib. Determine how long you want the straps to be and sew on a button on each strap. Finish the leg opening as previously described.

3½"
(9 cm)

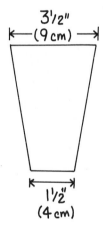

1½"
(4 cm)

BIB VARIATIONS

If you would like to have a front panel in a different color or design, cut a piece of fabric the length of the bib. The panel should be 3½" (9 cm) wide at the top and 1½" (4 cm) wide at the bottom. On the sides, press a ¼" (6 mm) seam allowance to the wrong sides. Place the panel at the middle of the bib and topstitch the sides close to the edges. Sew bib as previously described.

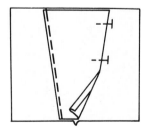
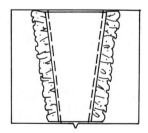

For a little fancier effect, you can add piping, eyelet, lace, etc., at the sides of the panel. These should be sewn in place at the same time you topstitch the panel.

APPLIQUES

Any applique on the bib will be very attractive. In Section 8 of this book are some suggestions, or you can create your own design. Any applique or design has to be applied to the front of the bib before you sew the bib together.

Another nice variation for the bib can be made by using the lines on the pattern for an overlap bib and combining different colors or prints. Use eyelet or lace for the edges of the bib. The pants can be long or short.

Use Master patterns:
    16 - Pants
    35 - Bib
    32 - Shoulder Straps

Trace pattern piece 35 following the lines for the overlap bib and the cutting lines for the LEFT and the RIGHT FRONT. Cut out two for the left front and cut two for the right front.

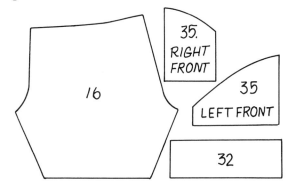

Sew on the applique to the left front, following instructions in Section 8.

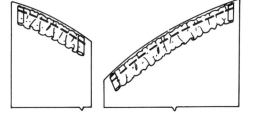

Cut two pieces of eyelet twice the length of the top edge of the left and right front. Sew gathering stitches ¼" (6 mm) from the raw edge of the eyelet and again in the middle of the seam allowance.

Pin the eyelet to the top edge of the bib with right sides and raw edges together. Pull up gathering stitches to fit and fold under ends of eyelet ¼" (6 mm). Sew on the eyelet.

Sew the shoulder straps as previously described.

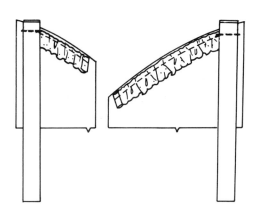

Pin the shoulder straps to the bib over the eyelet with edge of strap ¼" (6 mm) from the side edges of the bib. Sew across to keep in place.

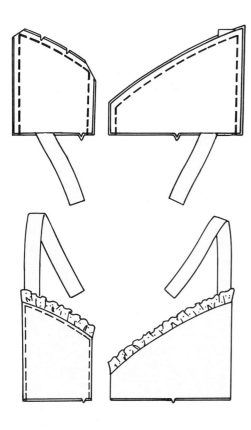

Pin the other front over the eyelet, right sides together, and sew the three sides. Be careful not to catch the eyelet with your stitches in the corners.

Trim corners. Turn right side out and press. Repeat for the right front. Topstitch right bib close to the edges as shown.

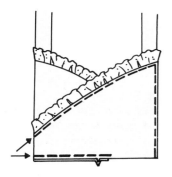

Overlap left bib over right bib, matching center front and sew together at waist to keep in place.

Topstitch close to the top edge of the bib as illustrated.

Finish the bib pants as previously described.

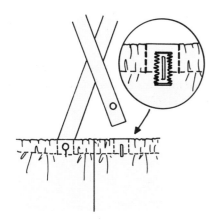

Mark position of the buttonholes on back at waist 1½" (4 cm) on each side of the center back seam.

Push the gathers away at buttonhole placement and sew across as shown.

Make the buttonholes. Sew on buttons to ends of straps to match the buttonholes.

Jumpsuits
Overalls
Dresses

7

A jumpsuit is especially practical for the child who is crawling or learning to walk. It eliminates the separation at the waist that occurs when a T-shirt and pants are worn. As is usually the case, the T-shirt has a tendency to crawl up, while the pants tend to slip down. Even suspenders on the pants do not solve this problem. It can be used for both boys and girls. The only difference is the color of the fabric. You can make a jumpsuit with either long or short sleeves. For the neck, you can use a simple neckband or a pretty collar. The pattern is designed with snaps at the crotch and on the inside of the legs, so that it will be easy to change the baby's diapers.

The front yoke of a jumpsuit is an excellent place to put a fancy applique, the baby's name, or some fancy embroidery. These tend to give the garment a very personal look, and jumpsuits finished in this manner make excellent gifts. You can be certain no one else has given the exact same gift.

A jumpsuit is a fun garment to construct when you use your imagination. The top and the sleeves can be made from a different color — even different textured fabric. Make imitation suspenders made with a contrasting color fabric. Just use your imagination, and you will marvel at the results.

This jumpsuit is designed with a zipper in the back. For a jumpsuit, we recommend that you use stretch velour, single knit, double knit or interlock.

Use Master patterns:
    25 - Lower Front
    26 - Front Bodice
    24 - Back
     3 - Sleeve
    28 - Collar
     6 - Cuffs for Long Sleeves, or
     7 - Bands for Short Sleeves

Be sure you cut out the pattern pieces on the lines marked "jumpsuit" on pattern pieces 24 and 26. You can cut on the cutting line for either short or long sleeves.

Fold the fabric double, right side to right side. Cut out the pattern pieces. The pattern includes ¼" (6 mm) seam allowance on all seams.

You need a 9" (23 cm) zipper for small and medium; 12" (30 cm) zipper for large and extra large.

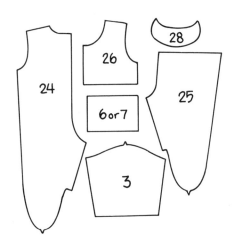

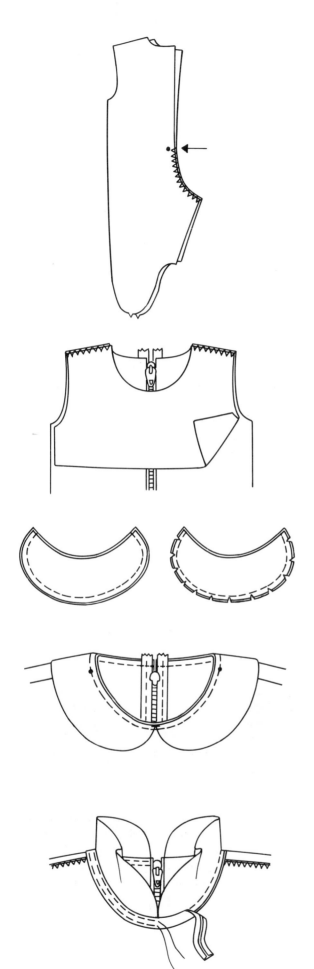

Mark the length of the zipper on the center back ½" (1.3 cm) down from the neckline. Sew the center back seam, stopping at this mark. Place a closed zipper on one side of the back, right side to right side, and ½" (1.3 cm) down from the neckline. Place the edge of the zipper tape even with the raw edges. Sew on the zipper as close as possible to the zipper teeth, using a zipper foot. Sew the other side using the same procedure.

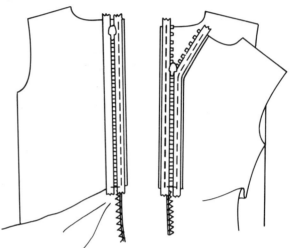

Sew the shoulder seams.

Place the collars, right side to right side, and sew around the outer edge, leaving the neckline open. Clip the seam allowances. Turn the collars right side out and press. Sew the collars together at the center front with a few stitches by hand on the seam allowance.

Mark the center front of the jumpsuit. Pin the collar on the right side of the neck opening matching center front with the ends of the collar at the center back. Match the dots on the collar to the shoulder seams. Sew on the collar through all layers.

An easy way to keep the raw edges flat is to topstitch around the neck opening through the seam allowances. The seam allowance should be away from the collar.

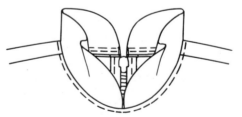

Another method is to place a piece of narrow bias tape over the seam allowance, fold under the ends of the tape, and topstitch as close as possible to the edge of the tape on both sides.

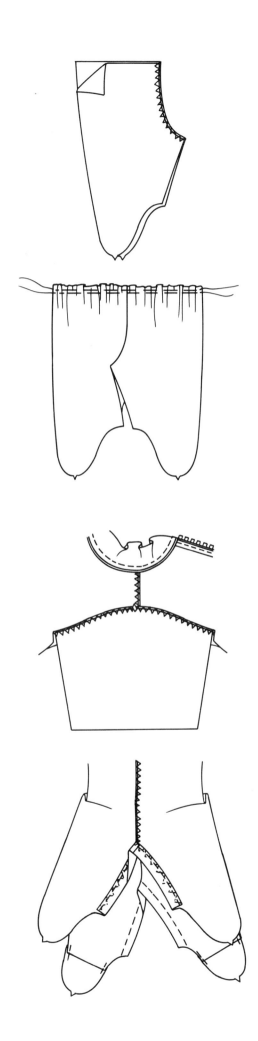

Sew the center front seam of the lower front. Fold two tucks on each side of the front between the marks on the patterns. Sew the tucks close to the edge to keep them in place.

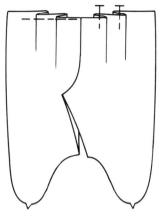

Instead of tucks, you may sew a gathering stitch. The gathered edge should be as wide as the bottom of the bodice. The gathered edge may have the gathers evenly placed or you may make a number of small gathers evenly spaced. Sew on the bodice to the lower front, right side to right side.

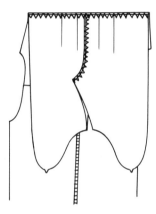

Sew in the sleeves by matching the underarm edges and the notch on the cap of the sleeve to the shoulder seam.

To make the foot, pin a tuck between the marks on the bottom of the back leg. This becomes the heel for the foot. Sew the tucks in place close to the edges.

Overcast the edges on the facing on both inside leg seams, both front and back. Press the facings to the wrong side on the folding line. Sew the facings close to the edges.

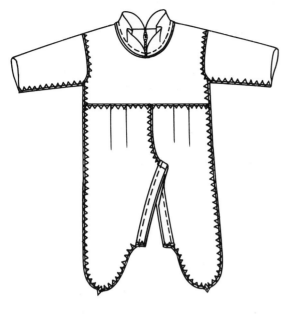

Place the back and front of the jumpsuit, right side to right side, matching the sleeve, the side seams and the foot up to the end of the facing. Sew the foot, side seam and sleeve in one continuous operation. Turn the jumpsuit right side out.

Apply snaps to the leg opening. The front leg opening should overlap the back.

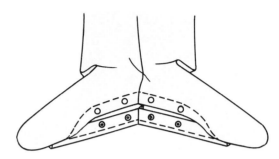

Finish the bottom of the sleeve by sewing on cuffs or sleevebands as previously described. Refer to page 44.

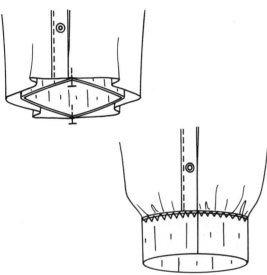

LEG CUFFS

If you do not want to have feet at the bottom of the legs, before you cut out the pattern, take this into consideration. Cut out the lower front and back on the line marked for cuffs. Use Master pattern 17 for the cuffs. Be sure to close the bottom snaps before you sew on the cuff. The seam on the cuff should be close to the inside leg seam, but not on it as it would make too much bulk at the leg seam.

JUMPSUIT WITHOUT SNAPS

If you do not wish to have snaps on the legs, change the pattern before you cut out the jumpsuit. Cut the pattern on the folding line at the inside legs to eliminate the facing. After you have sewn the side seams, sew the inside leg seams in one continuous operation.

JUMPSUIT WITH NECKBAND

If you would like to have a neckband instead of a collar, you have to sew the shoulder seams and apply the neckband before you sew on the zipper. Use Master pattern 14 for the neckband. This neckband will overlap at the center front. Add ¼" (6 mm) to the center back of the neckband. When you have cut out the neckband, cut it in half. Fold each piece lengthwise, wrong side to wrong side, and press. Mark the center front of the neck opening. Pin one band, right side to right side, to the neck opening extending ¼" (6 mm) over the center front. Match the center back. Do the same thing with the other half of the neckband; again, overlapping the center front. Sew on the neckband.

CENTER FRONT

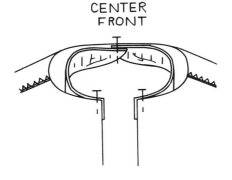

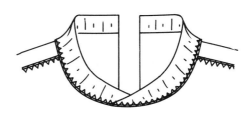

Sew on the zipper, turn under the ends of the zipper tape and secure with a few hand stitches.

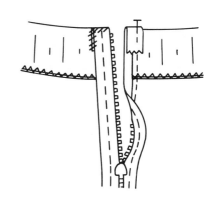

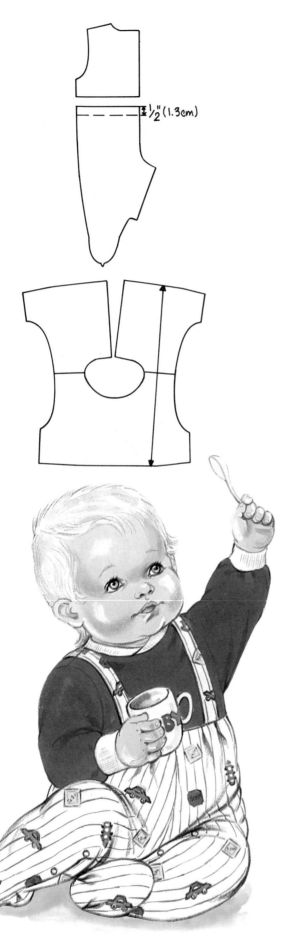

JUMPSUIT WITH CONTRASTING TOP

A jumpsuit can be made to look like a two-piece outfit by making the top part from contrasting fabric. Decorative suspenders can also be added.

Use the Master patterns listed on page 87 for a basic jumpsuit.

On back, pattern piece 24, cut the pattern apart on the line marked "dress". Add ½" (1.3 cm) to the lower portion of the back. Cut out the jumpsuit.

Sew the front bodice to the back bodice at the shoulder seams.

To make the decorative suspenders, cut two pieces of fabric 2½" (6.5 cm) wide and the length of the front and back bodice at placement shown on the illustration.

Fold the suspender double lengthwise, right sides together, and sew the long edge. Turn right side out and press. If desired, topstitch close to the edges. Place the suspenders to front and back bodice with right sides up and sew across the ends on front, back and shoulder seams to keep in place.

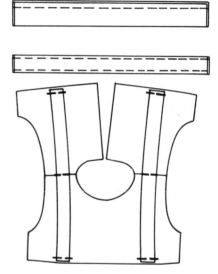

Sew upper part of back to lower part. Finish jumpsuit as described previously. Follow instructions on page 89.

PUFF SLEEVES

A little girl's jumpsuit looks very pretty when you make puff sleeves instead of regular sleeves, especially for a dress-up occasion. Use Master pattern 27 for the sleeves. How you construct puff sleeves, plus variations for the bottom edge, is described on page 98.

EYELET TRIM

A pretty variation for a little girl's jumpsuit can be made by finishing the neck opening with pregathered eyelet.

Cut one length of eyelet the length of the neck opening. Pin the right side of the eyelet to the right side of the neck opening. Fold under the ends at the center back. Sew on the eyelet using a ¼" (6 mm) seam allowance. If the eyelet has a bound edge, sew without catching the binding in the seam. After the eyelet is sewn, remove the binding to eliminate bulk.

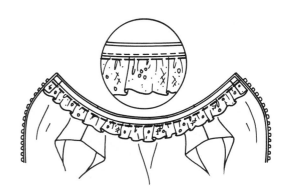

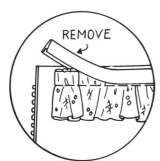

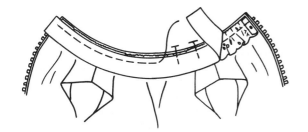

Finish the raw edges with self-fabric binding. Cut a piece of fabric 1" (2.5 cm) wide and the length of the neck opening plus ½" (1.3 cm). Pin the binding to the neck opening over the eyelet extending ends ¼" (6 mm). Sew in the same seam used for sewing on the eyelet. Fold the binding to the wrong side and fold under the ends. Topstitch ¼" (6 mm) from the seam. Trim off the excess length of binding.

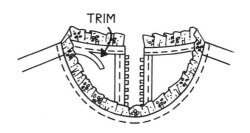

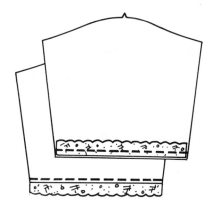

If you wish, you may trim the sleeves and the leg openings with the same eyelet. If you are using pregathered eyelet, we recommend that you remove the gathering before you sew on the eyelet as the elastic will do the gathering. If you are using eyelet for the legs, cut the pants 2" (5 cm) longer than the cutting line for cuffs marked on the pattern.

Place right side of the eyelet to the right side of the sleeves, and sew with a ¼" (6 mm) seam allowance. Overcast the seam allowance together. Fold the seam allowance toward the sleeve and sew through seam allowance and the sleeve close to the seam.

Apply the eyelet to the bottom of the legs using the same procedure.

Sew on the elastic to the sleeves by following the procedure on page 98.

OVERALLS

The construction of overalls is the same as that used for a jumpsuit. Overalls are usually worn over a T-shirt or a blouse, as they have deeper arm and neck openings.

Use Master patterns:
    25 - Lower Front
    24 - Back
    26 - Bodice
    29 - Neckband
    30 - Arm Opening Band

Make sure to cut pattern pieces 24 and 26 on lines for overalls.

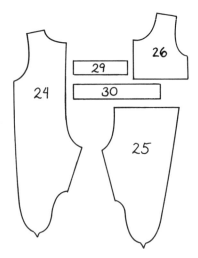

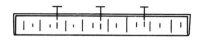

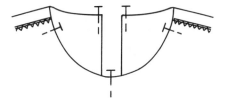

Sew bodice to lower front and sew the shoulder seams as previously described.

Press the neckband double, lengthwise, wrong side to wrong side. Divide the neckband and the neck opening into fourths with pins.

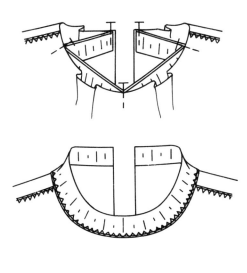

Pin the band to the neck opening on the right side with the raw edges together, matching the pins. The ends of the neckband should be at the center back. Sew on the neckband, stretching the band to fit the neck opening.

Sew on the zipper as previously described on page 88.

Sew the side seams first before you finish the arm openings.

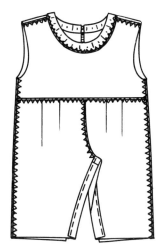

Sew the ends of the arm opening bands together to form circles. Fold each band double lengthwise, wrong sides together, and press. Divide the bands and the arm openings into fourths with pins.

Pin the bands to the arm openings right sides and raw edges together, matching the pins. Sew on the bands.

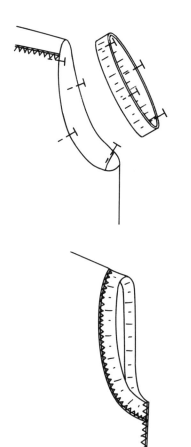

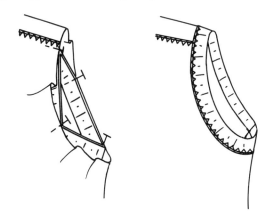

Another method for sewing on the arm opening bands is to sew on the band before you sew the side seam. When you are sewing the side seam, sew the ends of the band in one continuous operation.

DRESSES

There are times when a pretty little dress is very appropriate for a little girl. A dress gives you a perfect opportunity to use your creative imagination by using lace, trim, appliques, etc. You can create a "one of a kind" little dress. Dresses are a perfect gift item and they are always appreciated. You can make panties the same color as the dress, or you can use a different color for the panties and trim them with lace the same color as the dress. Use lightweight knits or lightweight woven fabric. Just remember that the fabric should be easy to care for as the little dress will be frequently washed.

While a plain cotton is the most commonly used fabric, there are many others which could be used to advantage. It is really fun to browse through a fabric store looking for the perfect material for an exquisite dress.

BASIC DRESS

We will first explain how to construct a basic dress, and this will be followed with a number of ideas on how the basic dress can be changed to give you a wide variety of styles.

For the basic dress, use Master patterns:

    24 - Back
    26 - Front Bodice
    27 - Sleeve
    28 - Collar

On pattern pieces 24 and 26, be sure to cut on the line marked for the dress.

Pattern piece 24 for the back bodice has to be adjusted to allow for a facing at the center back. At the center back, add 2¼" (5.5 cm) to the width.

The pattern piece for the skirt is not included in the Master pattern. The following measurements should be used for the skirt. These measurements include 1½" (4 cm) for the bottom hem.

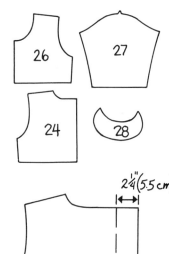

WIDTH:

Small	Medium	Large	Extra Large
36"	39"	42"	45"
(91.5 cm)	(99 cm)	(106.5 cm)	(115 cm)

LENGTH:

Small	Medium	Large	Extra Large
8"	9"	10"	11"
(20 cm)	(23 cm)	(25.5 cm)	(28 cm)

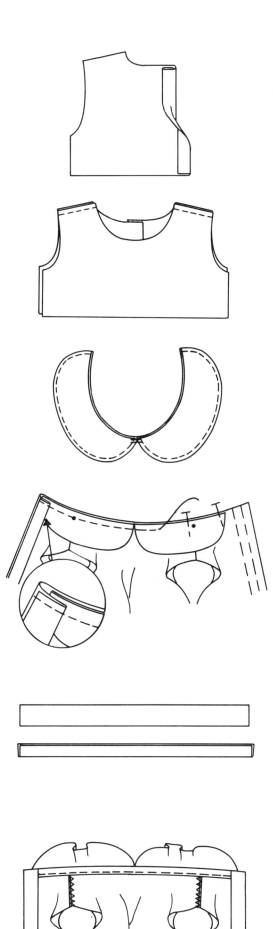

Place the fabric double, right side to right side, and cut out the pattern pieces.

Fold the back facing of the bodice twice to the wrong side 1" (2.5 cm) and press. There are now three layers of fabric on the facing. This is to stabilize the fabric when you make the buttonholes and sew on the buttons.

Sew the shoulder seams.

Place the collars, right side to right side, and sew around the outer edge, leaving the neckline open. Clip seam allowances. Turn the collars right side out and press. Topstitch around the collar close to the outer edge. Stitch the collar together at the center front with a few stitches by hand on the seam allowance.

Mark the center front of the dress. Pin the collar on the right side of the neck opening matching center front, dots to shoulder seams and with the ends of the collars at the center back, ½" (1.3 cm) from folding line (crease).

Fold the back facing on the folding line to the right side over the collar. Sew on the collar through all layers, including the facing in the seam.

The raw edges of the neck opening can be covered with self fabric or bias tape. For applying bias tape, follow the procedures described for the jumpsuit on page 88.

Instead of using bias tape to cover the raw edges, you may use self fabric. Cut a strip of fabric on the bias the length of the neck opening and 1¼" (3.2 cm) wide. Fold the strip double, lengthwise, wrong sides together. Place the strip on the collar with the raw edges of the strip and the collar together. Sew the strip to the collar on the same stitching line used to sew on the collar.

Cut off excess length of the bias strip. Fold the facing to the wrong side and fold the strip over the seam allowance. To keep the strip in place, topstitch close to the folded edge.

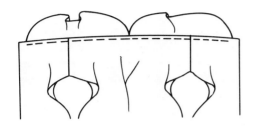

If you do not wish to cover up the raw edges with bias tape or self fabric, you can simply understitch the seam allowance to the neck opening.

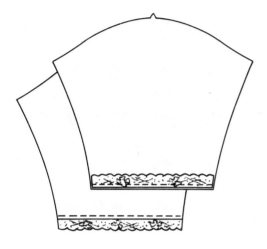

It is easier to finish the edges of the sleeves before you sew the sleeve seam. We suggest that you use a soft, narrow elastic ⅛" (3 mm) wide. Cut two strips of elastic 5" (12.5 cm) long.

You can either hem the bottom edge with a narrow hem or you can use lace. If you use lace, cut two strips of narrow lace the width of the sleeves. Place the lace, right side to right side, at the edge of the sleeve. Sew on the lace. Press the seam allowance toward the sleeve and topstitch close to the edge.

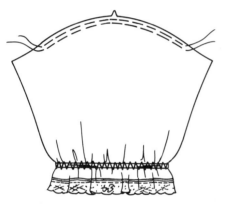

On the wrong side of the sleeve, sew on the elastic 1" (2.5 cm) up from the bottom edge of the sleeve. Stretch the elastic to fit the sleeve. Sew two rows of gathering stitches close together on the sleeve cap from mark to mark. Use long stitches with loose thread tension; pull the bobbin thread and gather as much as needed so that the sleeve will fit the sleeve opening.

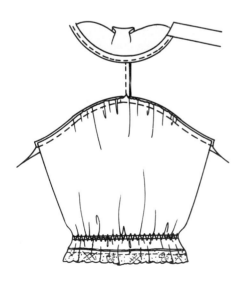

Sew on the sleeve, matching the notch on top of the cap to the shoulder seam, and the edges of the sleeves with the side seams. Sew the side seam and sleeve seam in one continuous operation.

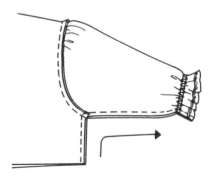

At each side of the skirt, fold the back facing 1" (2.5 cm) twice to the wrong side and press.

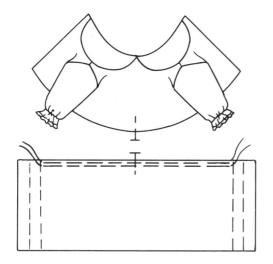

Mark the center front of the bodice and skirt. Sew two rows of gathering stitches close together on the top edge of the skirt. Pin the skirt to the bodice, right side to right side, matching the center front and back. Gather the skirt to fit the bodice. Be sure to adjust the gathers evenly. Do not have any gathers on the back facings. Sew on the skirt to the bodice.

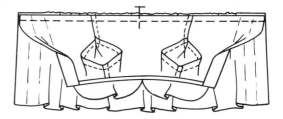

On the back, sew down the back facing close to the inner edge. Hem the dress.

Make buttonholes on the left back and sew on buttons to match the buttonholes.

COLLAR WITH LACE

We have described previously how to construct a collar. If you would like to alter the appearance of the dress, you can use a contrasting color or you can use lace on the edge.

If you are using lace, cut two strips of lace one and one-half times as long as the outer edge of the collars. Gather the lace so that it equals the outer edge of the collar. Sew on the lace to the outer edge of the collar. Place the collars right side to right side, sandwiching the lace between the collars with the raw edges together, and sew in the same line of stitching as for sewing on the lace.

Clip the seam allowances. Turn the collar right side out and you have a very pretty lace edging.

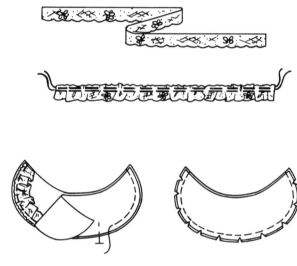

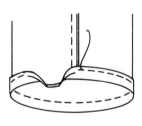

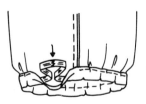

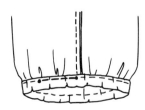

SLEEVES WITH ELASTIC IN CASING

Finish the bottom edge of the sleeve. Fold ⅝" (1.5 cm) to the wrong side for casing. Fold under the raw edges and sew close to the folded edge; leave an opening large enough to insert the elastic. To determine the length of the elastic, measure around the child's arm or wrist, and add 1" (2.5 cm). If you do not have the child's measurements, cut two pieces 6" (15 cm) long for long sleeves, or 7" (18 cm) long for short sleeves.

Insert elastic.

Overlap the ends of the elastic and sew them together. Finish sewing the casing seam.

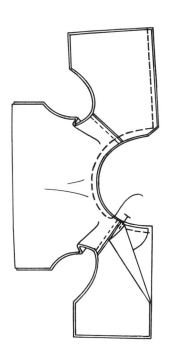

DOUBLE BODICE

If you are using a very lightweight fabric, you can make the front and back bodice with a double layer of fabric. This will produce a neater appearance on the inside. Use Master Pattern pieces listed on page 96. On back bodice pattern piece 24, add ½" (1.3 cm) to center back. Cut two layers for the front and back bodice.

Sew the shoulder seams for both layers. Make the collar as previously described.

Place the pieces, right side to right side, sandwiching the collar between the pieces. Sew the neck opening through all layers. Sew the center back. Clip corners. Turn the bodice right side out.

Finish the dress as previously described.

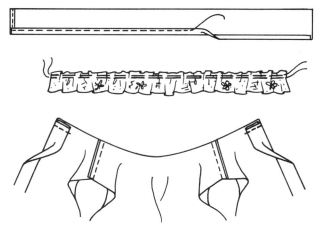

NECKLINE RUFFLE

A round neckline is very attractive if you add a ruffle; this is especially true if the ruffle is made using eyelet. Use eyelet approximately 1¼" (3 cm) wide and two times the length of the neck opening. A ruffle can also be made from a contrasting fabric or the same fabric as the dress. Cut the fabric 1½" (4 cm) wide. Hem one edge and the ends using a double narrow hem. Gather the unfinished edge of the ruffle. Sew front to back at shoulder seams. Fold the back facing twice to the wrong side 1" (2.5 cm), and sew across at the neck opening to keep in place.

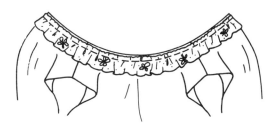

Divide the ruffle and the neck opening into fourths with pins.

Place the wrong side of the ruffle on the right side of the neck opening, raw edges together, with the ends of the ruffle on the folding line in the back. Match the pins and gather the ruffle to fit the neck opening. Sew on the ruffle using a ¼" (6 mm) seam allowance.

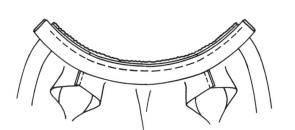

We suggest that you finish the neck opening with self-fabric binding. Cut a strip of fabric on the bias 2" (5 cm) wide and the length of the neckline plus 1" (2.5 cm). Fold the binding double lengthwise, wrong sides together. Pin the binding to the wrong side of the neck opening with all the raw edges together. The binding should extend ½" (1.3 cm) beyond the folding line in the back. Sew on the binding, using a ¼" (6 mm) seam allowance.

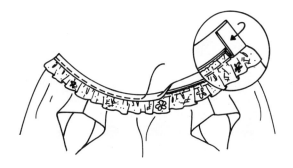

Fold under the ends of the binding. Fold the binding over the raw edges to the right side. Sew a straight stitch as close as possible to the fold.

TUCKS

Small tucks are very attractive on a baby's dress. The tucks can be at the front of the bodice or they can be on the skirt. On the bodice, the tucks look best if they are vertical; on the skirt, they look nicest if they are horizontal close to the bottom of the hem. When you are cutting out the skirt, allow sufficient fabric for the tucks. The following instructions tell how to make small tucks on the bodice.

The tucks should be sewn before you cut out the front bodice. The reason for this is that the tucks will change the size of the bodice. We recommend small tucks between ⅛" (3 mm) to ¼' (6 mm) wide and approximately ⅜" (1 cm) between the tucks. The easiest way to make tucks is to press the fabric, wrong side to wrong side, at the point where the folded edge of the tuck is located.

Sew the tucks with a straight stitch.

Sew six or eight tucks. Half the tucks should be pressed toward the right, the other half toward the left.

Leave a space approximately 1" (2.5 cm) at the center front. This space can be left plain or you can sew on a couple of pretty buttons.

Cut out the front bodice making sure that the center front is halfway between the right and the left tucks. Construct the dress as previously described.

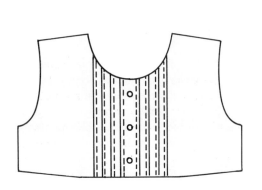

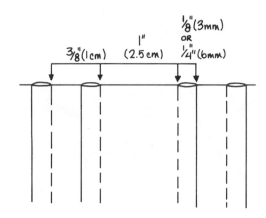

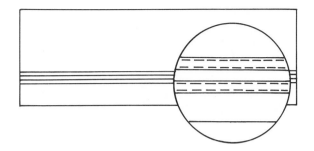

TRIMS

With the use of different colored ribbon or rickrack, you can create a very attractive dress. Cut the length of the ribbon the width of the skirt.

Pin the ribbon on the skirt and sew on the ribbon close to both edges. Using the same color ribbon, make small bows for the bodice. These can be sewn on by hand. If you wish to make stems for the bows, sew the pieces of ribbon to the bodice before attaching the skirt.

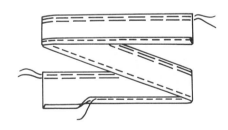

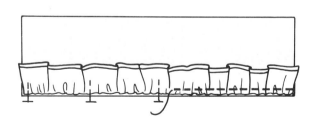

RUFFLES

A ruffle at the bottom of the skirt is easy to add. When you cut out the skirt, deduct 3½" (9 cm) from the length. Cut the ruffle approximately 2½" (6.5 cm) wide and twice the width of the skirt. Hem one long edge of the ruffle with a narrow hem. Or, you may wish to sew on some lace or eyelet. On the other side of the ruffle, sew two rows of gathering stitches.

Divide the bottom edge of the skirt and the top edge of the ruffle in fourths with pins.

Place the ruffle, right side to right side, on the bottom of the skirt. Match the pins, gather the ruffle to fit the bottom of the skirt, and sew on the ruffle.

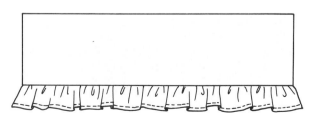

SUNDRESS

You can make a cute sundress with a ruffle at the bottom edge and the bodice trimmed with eyelet.

Use Master patterns:
    26 - Front Bodice
    24 - Back

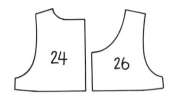

Adjust pattern piece 24. Cut the pattern on the line for dress for the back bodice and add ½" (1.3 cm) to center back. Trace the bodice on the lines for the overalls at the neck and arm openings. Cut two for the front bodice, cut four for the back bodice. Bodice will be double.

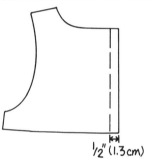

For the skirt, use the measurements given on page 96. If you wish to have the ruffle at the bottom edge, shorten the skirt 3½" (9 cm). Round the bottom edge of the skirt as illustrated. Cut out the skirt. Measure the bottom of the skirt and the back to the waist. Cut the ruffle 2½" (6.5 cm) wide and twice the length of the bottom of the skirt.

Sew the front bodice to the back bodice at the shoulder seams. Repeat.

Cut pieces of eyelet one and one-half times the length of the neck opening and the armholes.

Sew gathering stitches on the eyelet ¼" (6 mm) from edge and again in the middle of the seam allowance.

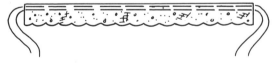

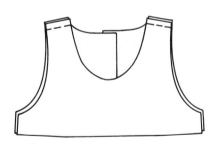

Pin the eyelet to neck opening with right sides together. Pull up gathering stitches to fit, adjusting gathers evenly. Fold under the ends of the eyelet ⅜" (1 cm).

Sew eyelet to the neck opening. Sew the eyelet to the arm opening using the same procedure.

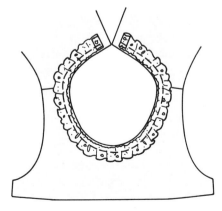

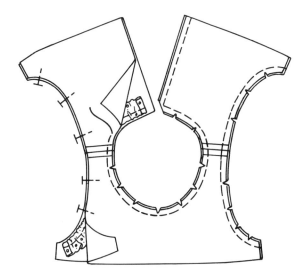

Pin the other bodice to bodice, right sides together, and sew the neck, arm openings, and back edges. Clip curved seam allowance, and trim corners.

Turn the bodice right side out as follows: Attach a safety pin to one layer of the back. Insert safety pin through the shoulder to the front and pull back to front. Repeat for the other back. Press.

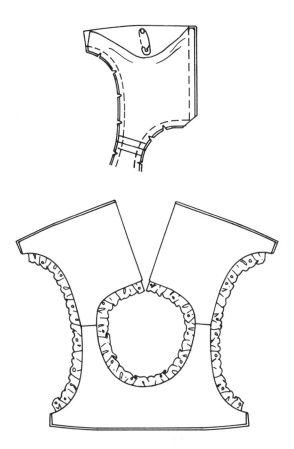

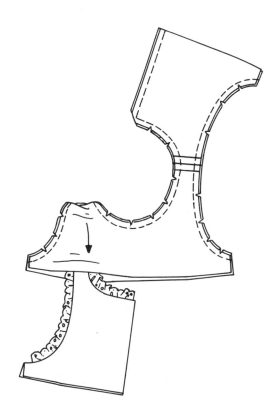

Sew front to back at side seams.

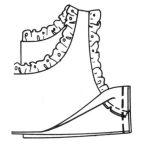

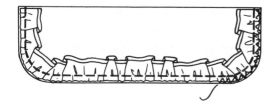

Hem the ruffle and sew gathering stitches as described on page 103.

Pin the ruffle to bottom edge of skirt with right sides together, matching center front and with ends of ruffle to waist edges of skirt. Pull up gathering stitches to fit, adjusting gathers evenly. Sew on the ruffle and overcast the raw edges together.

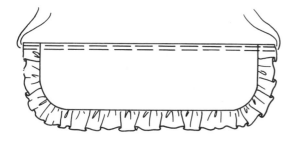

Sew gathering stitches on waist of skirt on seam line and again in the middle of the seam allowance.

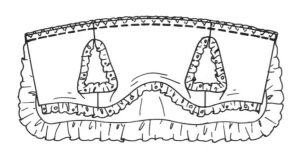

Pin skirt to bodice with right sides together, matching center front and ends of ruffle to edges of the back bodice. Pull up gathering stitches to fit, adjusting gathers evenly. Stitch.

Make buttonholes on left back bodice. Sew on buttons to match.

T-SHIRT DRESS

A T-shirt dress is one of the easiest dresses you can make and it is very pretty. Use a cotton knit or an interlock fabric.

Use Master patterns for the T-shirt for the bodice of the dress. Refer to page 42.

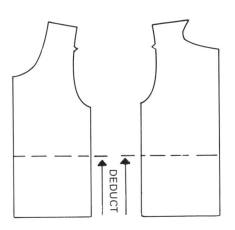

Shorten pattern pieces 1 and 2 the following amount:

Small	Medium
4½" (11.5 cm)	5" (12.5 cm)
Large	Extra Large
5½" (14 cm)	6" (15 cm)

Cut out the bodice. Cut out two pieces for the skirt, using the measurements given below:

LENGTH

Small	Medium	Large	Extra Large
8"	9"	10"	11"
(20 cm)	(23 cm)	(25.5 cm)	(28 cm)

WIDTH

Small	Medium	Large	Extra Large
18"	19"	20"	21"
(46 cm)	(49 cm)	(51 cm)	(54 cm)

Sew the bodice by following instructions for the T-shirt on page 42.

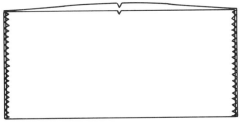

Sew the side seams of the skirt. Mark the center front and the center back of the skirt and bodice with small clips or a water soluable pen. Sew gathering stitches on waist of skirt ¼" (6 mm) from edge and again in the middle of the seam allowance.

Pin the skirt to the bodice, matching center front, center back, and match the side seams. Pull up gathering stitches to fit the waist, adjusting gathers evenly. Stitch.

Fold up 1½" (4 cm) hem and press. Hem skirt by topstitching close to inner edge of hem or blind hem.

RUFFLES AT ARM OPENINGS

Sew the bodice of the dress up to the point of sewing in the sleeves. Cut two pieces of fabric 8" (20 cm) long on lengthwise grain and 1¾" (4.5 cm) wide. Round off the ends of the ruffles as illustrated.

On the straight edge of each ruffle, fold a narrow hem to the wrong side and stitch. Sew gathering stitches on the other side of the ruffle ¼" (6 mm) from edge and again in the middle of the seam allowance.

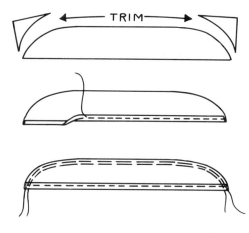

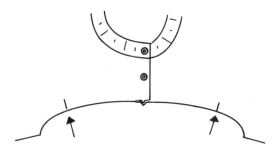

On arm opening of bodice, mark 2½" (6.5 cm) from shoulder on front and back.

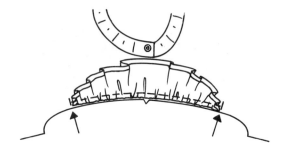

Pin ruffle to arm opening, right sides and raw edges together, placing ends of ruffle at marks. Pull up gathering stitches to fit, adjusting gathers evenly. Stitch.

Finish bodice as previously described.

Appliques Monograms Sleeping Bag

SECTION

8

Cute and pretty appliques make fun decorations for baby and toddlers' clothes. They can be used on sleepers, bibs, dresses; in fact, on almost everything! You can use your imagination to decorate and personalize any outfit or item. Appliques can be applied to both knit and woven fabric. In addition to being fun, they are also easy to make. You can use scrap pieces of fabric for the appliques; these also can be from knit or woven fabric. It is nice to coordinate the applique with the garment. For example, if you are making a T-shirt and pants, and you would like to have the applique on the T-shirt, use the pants fabric for the applique. Appliques can be made from one color fabric or you can add other colors of fabric for detail areas. Buttons, metal eyelets, rickrack, narrow ribbons and any trim can be used to add detail to the applique.

Start collecting the scraps of fabric that are suitable for appliques; a box for prints and a box for solids. You will be amazed how often you will use these scraps.

A good source of ideas for appliques are children's story books and coloring books. Trace the designs on tissue paper. You can simplify the designs by eliminating any unnecessary lines.

For soft or lightweight fabrics, we recommend interfacing the fabric pieces with a lightweight fusible interfacing. The interfacing will make the applique a little stiffer, but it will be easier to sew especially if you are using a knit fabric or a fabric which ravels.

Press the interfacing to the wrong side of the fabric pieces which will be used for the applique. Transfer the design to the fabric, and cut out the applique.

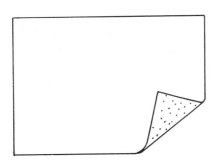

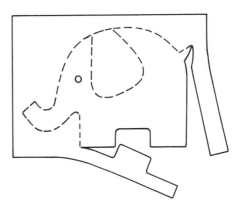

Place the applique on the garment. Secure with small pieces of fusible webbing, glue stick or baste the applique to the garment with hand or machine stitches.

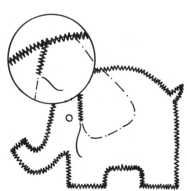

Stabilize the garment under the position of the applique to prevent puckering when sewing on the applique. For stabilizing, use paper, or a "tear away material" which is made especially for this use.

Sew over all the raw edges using a close stitch length and a medium to wide zigzag stitch. Try stitching on a scrap of the same fabric and adjust the stitch length and width. Adjust the length of the stitches so that the fabric does not show through and the stitches are not piled up. Loosen the top thread tension so that the top thread is pulled to the underside and the bobbin thread does not show on the right side. Tear away the stabilizing material on the wrong side, after the applique is completed.

If you are applying an applique to a garment made from terry or velour, or any other fabric with nap or texture, the following method works very well.

Draw or copy the design you wish to use on the fabric for the applique. Pin the fabric with the applique to the garment. Sew around the outside edges of the design, using a narrow zigzag stitch or a straight stitch.

Trim away the excess fabric as close as possible to the stitches. Stabilize the garment under the position of the applique as previously described. Now sew around the edges of the design again, using a wide zigzag stitch and the stitches closer together.

If you are using an applique with more than one color, such as a train engine, draw the engine on one piece of fabric, cut out the various colors for the windows, wheels, etc. It is easier to sew on the various parts if you either glue them on with a glue stick, or use a very small piece of fusible webbing between say the wheel and the fabric. Use a warm iron to fuse the pieces together. Place the applique at the desired spot and sew on the applique. Sew around the various parts with a close zigzag stitch, over the raw edges. Any small detail can always be embroidered by hand.

Letters, or numbers such as "1, 2, 3" and "ABC" are often seen on small children's clothes. These are sewn on using the same techniques as used for applying appliques.

An easy way to make appliques is to use fabric with an adhesive back. When using this type of fabric, cut out the applique before you sew it on. Press it on the right side of the fabric, and then sew just once around the outer edges. If you do not sew around the edges, the applique will come off with repeated launderings.

You can find an unlimited supply of ready-made appliques in most fabric stores. These you just sew on by hand.

BUNNY APPLIQUE

A cute design can be made by placing part of the applique on the front and part on the back. If you would like to put the applique on a sweatshirt, be sure to cut the back in two pieces, adding a seam allowance to the center back.

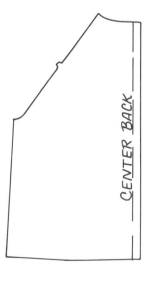

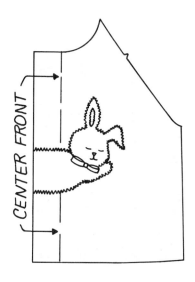

Sew the applique to the front and to the back. Now sew the center back seam. Tie a bow and attach to the neckline with hand stitches. Attach a pom-pom for the tail.

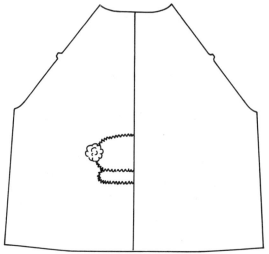

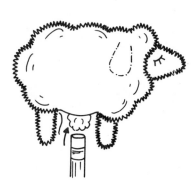

PADDED APPLIQUE

A padded applique gives more emphasis to the design. Leave a small opening when sewing on the applique. Insert the batting through the opening. An easy way to do this is to use the eraser end of a pencil. Finish by sewing the opening.

OUTLINING

A pretty design can be made on a garment with outline stitching. Copy the design to a tear-away material or tissue paper. Position the design on the garment. Sew over the lines with a straight stitch to transfer the design to the garment. Tear away the paper.

Place a piece of stabilizing material on the wrong side of the garment under the position of the design. Using a satin stitch, sew over the straight stitches. Tear away the stabilizing material on the wrong side.

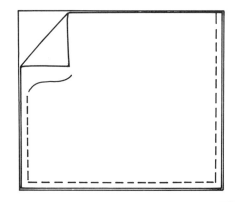

WALL HANGING FOR THE NURSERY

By using appliques, you can create a very colorful and interesting wall hanging. You can use almost any kind of fabric. Decide on the size and cut out the fabric. Press on interfacing on the back of the fabric. Cut out the pictures or design in various colors. Felt is a good fabric for this as the edges do not unravel. You may glue on the designs using special glue which you can obtain from your fabric store, or you can place fusible webbing behind the designs and press them on. Or, you may sew on the designs. Use a piece of cardboard for the back or place the wall hanging over stretcher bars. Pull the fabric so it is taut and staple to the back of the bars.

If you are using cardboard, cut another piece of fabric the same size as the picture. Place the two pieces, right side to right side, and sew the three sides, leaving the top edge open. Turn the fabric right side out. Insert a piece of cardboard and close the top opening. Attach a ribbon or a string at each top corner so that you can hang the picture.

For a smaller picture, you may eliminate the cardboard as the press-on interfacing will make the picture stiff enough to hang properly. To make a picture more interesting, you may wish to sew around the edge using a fancy stitch, lace or rickrack.

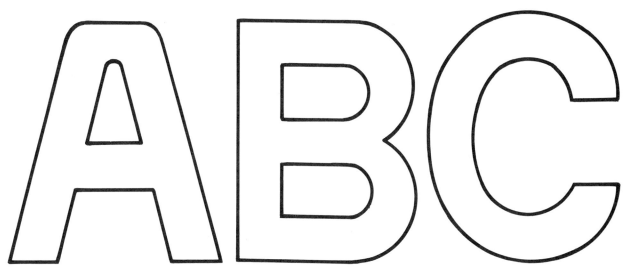

117

SLEEPING BAG

It used to be a tremendous amount of work and trouble to travel with a baby. You had to load up with extra diapers, blankets, extra bottles, etc. While it is still work to travel with a baby, it is nothing like it used to be. Now you can buy disposable diapers, disposable bottles of premixed formulas, disposable nipples, etc. In fact, you throw so much away that you have to be careful you do not throw away the baby! You still do not throw away the blankets, but you can have the next best thing: a baby sleeping bag. Made out of quilted fabrics—non-allergic, nylon outside, quilted with polyester filling, completely machine washable and machine dryable, it folds into a small package, and weighs almost nothing. In fact, it is the perfect item to take some of the work and trouble out of taveling with a baby.

The quilted fabric for a sleeping bag comes in various weights. The weight means the thickness of the filling. You determine the weight according to the conditions under which the sleeping bag will be used. The fabric usually runs from 4 to 12 oz. (100 g to 300 g).

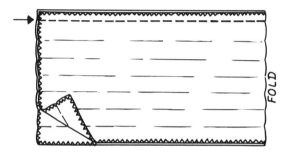

Cut a rectangular piece of fabric 27" (70 cm) wide and 90" (230 cm) long. Overcast all raw edges to keep the filling in place. Fold the fabric double, lengthwise, right side to right side. Pin one of the long sides together. Sew a seam 1½" (4 cm) from the raw edge.

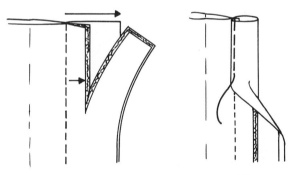

Trim the seam allowance to ⅝" (1.5 cm) except for the bottom layer of nylon which should be left 1½" (4 cm) wide. Now, fold this seam allowance over the raw edges and fold under the seam allowance edge. Sew in place.

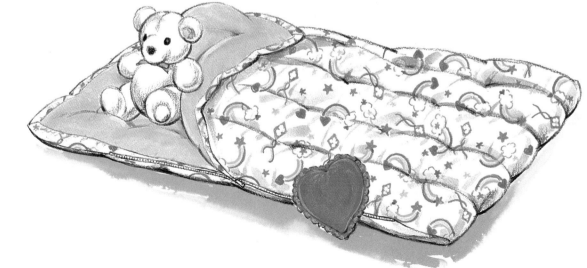

119

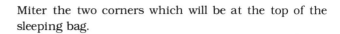

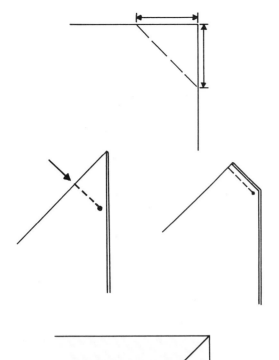

Miter the two corners which will be at the top of the sleeping bag.

To miter the corners, measure 3" (7.5 cm) from the corners on each side. Mark with pins or chalk. On the wrong side of the fabric, draw a line across from mark to mark.

Fold the corner double, right side to right side, and sew a seam on the line, stopping ¼" (6 mm) from edge.

Trim the excess fabric and turn the corners right side out.

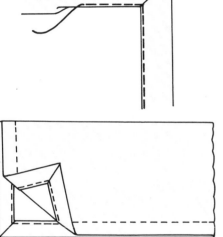

On the top and the sides where the opening will be, pin a 1½" (4 cm) hem to the wrong side. Fold under the raw edge ¼" (6 mm) and sew.

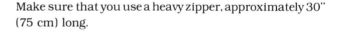

Make sure that you use a heavy zipper, approximately 30" (75 cm) long.

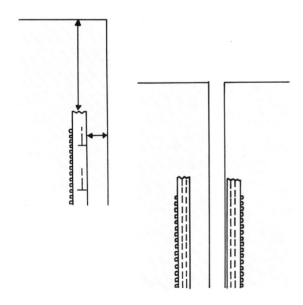

Place the zipper on the right side of the sleeping bag 10" (25 cm) down from the top edge and 1½" (4 cm) in from the edge. The edge of the zipper tape should face the opening. Be sure that the right side of the zipper is on the right side of the fabric. Pin the zipper in place. The zipper will not go all the way to the bottom of the bag. Sew a seam close to the edge of the zipper tape. Sew a second seam ¼" (6 mm) in from the first seam. Open the zipper.

Measure the distance from the top of the bag to where the zipper starts. Measure the same distance on the other side. Start pinning the other part of the zipper at this point, right side to right side, with the zipper tape even with the edge of the fabric.

Sew one seam close to the edge of the zipper tape and a second seam ¼" (6 mm) in from this seam.

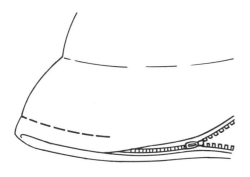

Close the zipper and turn the sleeping bag right side out. Close the opening between the bottom of the zipper and the bottom of the bag by sewing a seam from the end of the zipper to the bottom of the bag. The two edges will not be even.

You must be sure that the sleeping bag is not too long or the baby will have a tendency to slide to the bottom. You do not want to make a new sleeping bag every time the baby grows a few inches. To overcome this problem, you can make a sleeping bag that grows with the baby. Determine how long you want the sleeping bag to be. Using a long straight stitch sew across the bag at this point. When the baby grows, simply rip out the stitches and sew another seam further down.

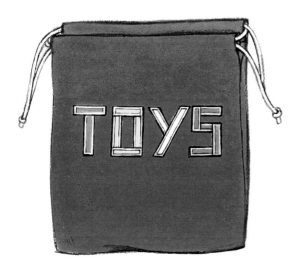

TOY BAG

When you are traveling with a baby, it is very convenient to have a small tote bag to carry a few of the baby's toys. Cut a piece of sturdy fabric 24" (61 cm) long and 8" (20 cm) wide. If you want the baby's name or an applique on the bag, do this before you construct the bag.

If you would like to have a larger bag, cut a piece of fabric 36" (90 cm) long and 15" (35 cm) wide.

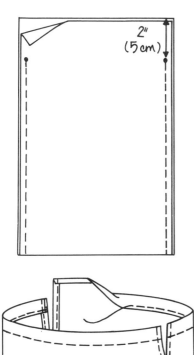

Fold the fabric double lengthwise, right sides together. Sew the side seams starting 2" (5 cm) from the top. At the top of the sides seams, hem the raw edges by turning ¼" (6 mm) to the wrong side.

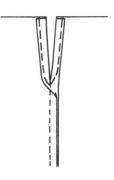

Fold the top opening over to the wrong side 1" (2.5 cm), fold under the raw edge and hem around the opening.

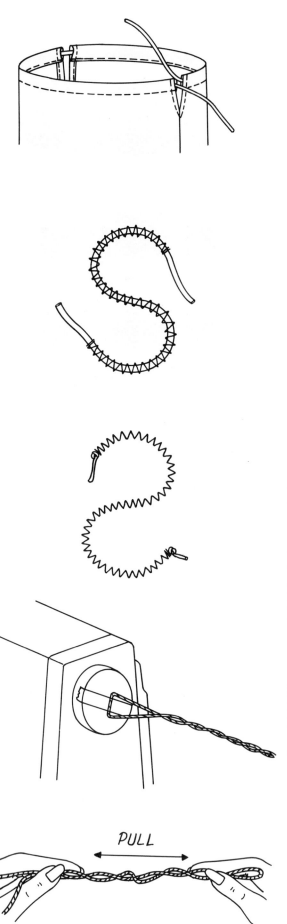

For the drawstring, cut two strings 20" (51 cm) long. Thread the strings through the openings on each side of the bag as shown. Knot the two strings together on each side.

If making the larger bag, cut the drawstrings 36" (90 cm) long.

MONOGRAMS

Some of the most modern sewing machines are programed to make monograms. Some can even write letters and names; however, most machines cannot perform these functions. If your sewing machine can perform these functions, refer to your instruction book for details.

For a very attractive monogram on stretch terry or terry cloth for a bath blanket, use a piece of yarn in a contrasting color. Start at one end of an initial leaving a few inches of yarn at the beginning. Sew on the yarn using a zigzag stitch. This stitch should be wide enough so that it misses the yarn. Follow the outline of the initial; again leave a piece of extra yarn at the end.

Pull the ends of the yarn to the wrong side and make a knot as close as possible to the fabric. The knots will keep the yarn in place.

To make a thicker yarn, cut one long piece of yarn, divide it in half, and tape the middle of the yarn to the center of the handwheel of your sewing machine. Hold the ends in your hand and slowly run the machine. This will twist the yarn pieces together to form a thicker yarn. Now, fold the yarn in half. It will twist together by itself the other way. Straighten the yarn. Use this yarn to form the monogram, sew it on using a zigzag or a blind hem stitch.

PULL

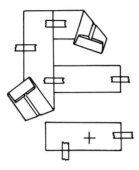

You can also make monograms using bias tape. Cut the pieces of bias tape to be used for the letter. For example, if you are making an "E", you will have one long piece of bias tape and three small pieces. Tuck under the edges of the long piece and tape or pin in position. Fold under one end on each of the three small pieces. Tuck the other end of the small piece under the long piece as illustrated. Tape or pin in place and sew a zigzag stitch around all the outer edges.

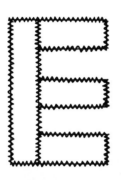

YARDAGE REQUIREMENTS
Yardage requirements are for basic garments only.
For variations, use these only as a guide.
Notions are not listed, purchase notions accordingly.

Sleeper or Kimono

STRETCH KNITS ONLY
with 25% Stretch across
the grain
Suggested Fabrics: Stretch
terry, interlock

Fabric 60" (152 cm) wide: 1 yd (0.95 m)
Ribbing 28" (71 cm) wide: 5" (12 cm)

T-shirt or Rugby Shirt

STRETCH KNITS ONLY
with 18% Stretch across
the grain
Suggested Fabrics: Single
knit, interlock

Fabric 60" (152 cm) wide: ½ yd (0.50 m)
Ribbing 28" (71 cm) wide: Short sleeve - 3" (7 cm)
Long sleeve - 5" (12 cm)

Panties

STRETCH KNITS ONLY
with 18% Stretch across
the grain
Suggested Fabrics: Single
knit, interlock

Fabric 60" (152 cm) wide: ½ yd (0.50 m)
Ribbing 28" (71 cm) wide: 3" (7 cm)

Romper

STRETCH KNITS ONLY
with 18% Stretch across
the grain
Suggested Fabrics: Single
knit, interlock

Fabric 60" (152 cm) wide: ⅝ yd (0.60 m)
Ribbing 28" (71 cm) wide: 5" (12 cm)

Jogging Suit

STRETCH KNITS ONLY
Suggested Fabrics:
Sweatshirt fleece, stretch
velour, double knit

Fabric 60" (152 cm) wide: 1 yd (0.95 m)
Ribbing 28" (71 cm) wide: 7" (18 cm)

Sweatshirt

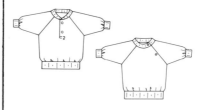

STRETCH KNITS ONLY
Suggested Fabrics:
Sweatshirt fleece, stretch
velour, double knit

Fabric 60" (152 cm) wide: ½ yd (0.50 m)
Ribbing 28" (71 cm) wide: 9" (23 cm)

Pants

Firm knit or light to
medium weight woven
fabric
Suggested Fabrics: Double
knit, cotton types

Fabric 45" (115 cm) wide: ⅝ yd (0.60 m)
Fabric 60" (152 cm) wide: ⅝ yd (0.60 m)

Sweatshirt with Hood

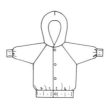

STRETCH KNITS ONLY
Suggested Fabrics:
Sweatshirt fleece, stretch
velour, double knit

Fabric 60" (152 cm) wide: ⅝ yd (0.60 m)
Ribbing 28" (71 cm) wide: 9" (23 cm)

Dress with Short or Long Sleeves

Lightweight woven fabric
Suggested Fabrics: Cotton types

Fabric 45" (115 cm) wide: ⅞ yd (0.80 m)

T-shirt Dress with Short or Long Sleeves

STRETCH KNITS ONLY
with 18% stretch across the grain
Suggested Fabrics: Single knit, interlock

Fabric 60" (152 cm) wide: ⅝ yd (0.60 m)
Ribbing 28" (71 cm) wide: Short sleeve - 3" (7 cm)
Long sleeve - 5" (12 cm)

Short Pants

Firm knit or lightweight woven fabric
Suggested Fabric: Single knit, cotton types

Fabric 60" (152 cm) wide: ⅜ yd (0.35 m)
Fabric 45" (115 cm) wide: ⅜ yd (0.35 m)

Short Bib Overalls

Firm knit or light to medium weight woven fabric
Suggested Fabrics: Double knit, cotton types

Fabric 60" (152 cm) wide: ½ yd (0.50 m)
Fabric 45" (115 cm) wide: ⅝ yd (0.60 m)

Jumpsuit

STRETCH KNITS ONLY
Suggested Fabrics: Double knit, stretch velour, single knit, sweatshirt fleece

Fabric 60" (152 cm) wide: 1 yd (0.95 m)

Bib Overalls

Firm knit or light to medium weight woven fabric
Suggested Fabrics: Double knit, cotton types

Fabric 60" (152 cm) wide: ¾ yd (0.70 m)
Fabric 45" (115 cm) wide: ⅞ yd (0.80 m)
Ribbing 28" (71 cm) wide: 5" (12 cm)

Jumpsuit with Contrast Top

STRETCH KNITS ONLY
Suggested Fabrics: Double knit, stretch velour, single knit, sweatshirt fleece

Fabric 60" (152 cm) wide: Top - ⅜ yd (0.35 m)
Pants - ¾ yd (0.70 m)

Overalls

STRETCH KNITS ONLY
Suggested Fabric: Double knit, stretch velour, single knit, sweatshirt fleece

Fabric 60" (152 cm) wide: ⅝ yd (0.60 m)
Ribbing 28" (71 cm) wide: 7" (17 cm)

Comforter

Fabric 45" (115 cm) wide: 3 yd (2.75 m)

Bumper Pads

45" (115 cm) wide woven fabric: 1⅛ yd (1.05 m) of two colors OR 2¼ yd (2.10 m) of one color

MASTER PATTERN PIECES INCLUDED

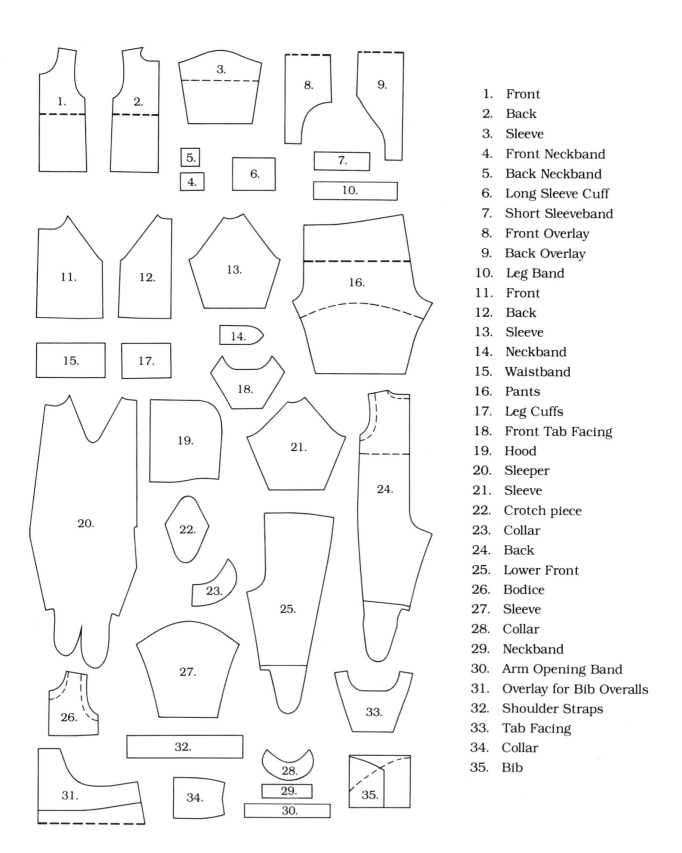

1. Front
2. Back
3. Sleeve
4. Front Neckband
5. Back Neckband
6. Long Sleeve Cuff
7. Short Sleeveband
8. Front Overlay
9. Back Overlay
10. Leg Band
11. Front
12. Back
13. Sleeve
14. Neckband
15. Waistband
16. Pants
17. Leg Cuffs
18. Front Tab Facing
19. Hood
20. Sleeper
21. Sleeve
22. Crotch piece
23. Collar
24. Back
25. Lower Front
26. Bodice
27. Sleeve
28. Collar
29. Neckband
30. Arm Opening Band
31. Overlay for Bib Overalls
32. Shoulder Straps
33. Tab Facing
34. Collar
35. Bib

A ¼" (6 mm) seam allowance is included on all pattern pieces.

Notes